I Never Walked Alone

Hope you enjoy the Journey! R.H.

Jerry Hale

by

Jerry Hale

Copyright © by Jerry Hale

Canadian Cataloguing in Publication Data
Hale, Jerry, 1940-
    I never walked alone

ISBN 1-55056-494-3

    1. Hale, Jerry, 1940- 2. Alberta--Biography. 1. Title.
FC3675.1.H34A3 1998 971.23'03'092   C98-910026-X

Published by Jerry and Rose Hale
Box 233
Worsley, Alberta
T0H 3W0

First printing 1997
Second printing 1997
Third printing 1998

Printed and bound in Canada by
Friesens Corporation,
Altona, Manitoba

CONTENTS

Foreword

Imagine taking a time machine back to the nineteen twenties or even further. Imagine that there are few cars, fewer people, no appliances to plug in and no power even if there was an appliance.

Would a time traveller stay or opt for something else?

This book argues there is nothing better. The author is very honest about the conditions he endured. He records life the way he lived it: like a tapestry.

People come, they contribute what they know and they leave. If they are really important, they show up again. Some people interest us, some do not. Almost everyone uniquely defines who they are and what contribution they make to his life.

Nothing escapes a child's wonder and all are equally important. Boys have courage that men do not. A boy thinks nothing of the consequences of a skunk spraying him. He merely wants to get the skunk out of his way, so he kicks him off a bridge. The smell is everyone else's problem, not his.

Rams, rats, dogs who travel in packs and kill chickens, neighbours who deny their dog's involvement, horses that hate gravel and run like their tail is on fire, hounds that live in an abandoned farm house that the family will move into, goats who eat anything (and become supper when they do it once too often), are what populates a child's world. And events good or bad are all held together by family and family values.

The author never tells us exactly what he thinks of his father, but the stories do. His father was a man of principle who never wavered from what he believed was right. A son could be made to believe he could spend a night in jail for being uncivil towards his mother. His father was never to be disobeyed and responsibility was to work hard, guide the family, make difficult decisions and live by them.

He sees his mother as steady and unflappable. She is capable of understanding at the deepest level what is important and what is not. She seldom needs to discipline her children because she has other bonds that are deeper and much more effective. When she speaks, it is with a deep authority which defies disobedience.

These two people, their values and a simple acceptance and obedience to God's will are the reoccurring themes that mold a Christian. Every story told serves in our understanding of God's way, though it may not be directly stated.

The middle section of the book shows life in rural Canada. I live in the same community the author writes about, and I can tell you my life has been nothing like what he describes. We have paved roads, electricity, modern schools, touch tone telephones, satellite dishes, modern tractors, and village water and sewage. Hardship to me is the power going off, its -40o C and I have to walk two blocks to work. I cannot imagine not having power at all. I cannot imagine getting water from a well or a dugout. I cannot imagine unloading coal in the morning and giving birth the same day in the evening.

Nor do I know people who want to get away from the farm so badly that they would shoot their dog to feed the pigs while they are gone. I do not know anyone who would be thoughtful enough to phone everyday to check on my children and keep them on the phone until my wife returned from her chores. I think it a great lesson to read of a farmer who wanted to return more to the land than he took and that before environmental issues were well publicized. The people and places Mr. Hale writes about are about as alien as to me as space itself. One cannot read about it without wishing for the wonderful rewards Mr. Hale receives.

The third section of I Never Walked Alone has to do with "working out". Though the reader may not be familiar with the exact nature of the jobs, several things become apparent. One is how much work it takes to maintain a farm in marginal farming country. There is no such thing as a winter vacation on Southern California beaches. Winter is just as hard as summer. Maybe worse. People from the south should come up and try and breath in a -50oC day. It is like having hot lead pored down one's throat. One cannot imagine the pain of being in severe cold, let alone working in it.

Many stories have been told about banks and farming. The point of this one is that everything was lost, but with patience and a little understanding on the banks part, the tragedy could have been averted. So often we judge things without understanding their underlying merit. The bank needed only to guide the Hales; it did not have to become so antagonistic so quickly.

The last part of I Never Walked Alone is a welcome reprieve. ard work is never wasted. The Hales wind up in Cassiar region of British Columbia. They begin their lives again. And they begin with the same courage, same values, same determination, and same simple faith that they began with.

And those of us who know their story, would not want to live it, but we admire them for the warm and thoughtful people their life has made them.

Jerome Cherry
Worsley, Alberta,   January 19, 1995

Introduction

I would trust my life in Jerry's hands, but our relationship did not begin that way. The seeds of character were planted when he was a child and Jerry developed them over the years through happiness, pain and sorrow by the choices he has made.

I met Jerry when we were teenagers when they first moved to Worsley, Alberta, Canada. I was intrigued with the foreign language he spoke at that time. (He was from Texas!) Texas lost a good son and Canada gained a good man!

When we introduced ourselves, it was a good kindred feeling right from the beginning. The Lord knew I would need a good and true friend and Jerry has been one throughout time.

We were both raised in Christian homes, but from two different church backgrounds. "Paul or Apollos" that has never bothered Jerry. His only concern was "How is your walk with the Lord?" or "Do you know Him?" or "Do you call upon Him for help?"

I never have met a man as focused as Jerry in talking about what the Lord can do in our lives. He would ask in such a way that you knew he really cared and is able to make you aware of what you are doing with your life.

One time, he asked me if I had made a commitment to lead one soul to the Lord this year. It sure made me aware of what I was doing.

His intent of correction is not to point a finger, but to lend a hand. As you read this book, you will see that. Jerry can laugh a little and cry a little. He also has had many problems and successes, that through choice, allowed the hand of the Lord to guide him throughout his life. If you could get to meet him and be his friend, you would be very rich.

Thank you Jerry for being my friend and mentor.
Ken Rohl
Calgary, Alberta, Canada

Dedication

I would like to dedicate this book to:

My wife, Rose who has stood with me; not in front of me or behind me, but beside me for the past thirty-five years. For the hardship she has gone through to help support me because she believed in me; for helping me to teach our children to have faith in the Lord; for exercising her strength, endurance, faithfulness, and encouragement. Truly a great woman is priceless to her man - my wife is truly a great woman. She has spent endless hours helping me put this together.

My children, that have been so much help down through the years and who have made me so proud to be their Dad. As I have tried to do down through the years, my children are trying to take good care of the family name that has been given them.

Acknowledgments

I have a great appreciation for the following people for encouraging me to put this book together:

First for an old friend who encouraged me to put some history together of my family life in Texas and moving to the great country of Canada. Robert Fielder has now gone to be with the Lord.

Wade Davis and his wife, Gail were also a great encouragement to me to push on and get this project completed. They reassured me it would not be time wasted.

To Jo and Roy Somers, sister and brother-in-law, for the many hours of work and dedication, making sure all the I's were dotted and the T's crossed. All the hours of instruction and encouragement they gave to my Rose on the computer was much appreciated.

Finally to Jerome Cherry for the work he did in helping, especially in the outline and summary.

Chapter One
Precious Mem'ries

In the magnificent Cassiar mountain range of Northwest British Columbia, Canada, almost midway on Highway 37, at Tatogga Lake, I stopped with my arms full of wood, to look at the thermometer on the post.

The mercury was almost at the bottom sitting on a minus fifty. The lake had been cracking all day from the ice and I knew it was cold, but inside this old log house with the wood heater crackling and popping it was nice and warm.

Outside the window, the long icicles hung with a little glitter in them as twilight turned into darkness. Somewhere away across the lake upon the side of the mountain, a lonesome call from a timber wolf made old Spike's ears perk up. Rose had said, "Why don't we let him sleep inside tonight, it's so cold out there."

The wood box was full and an old coat lay by the door to stop any cold from coming in. We had just finished a fresh feed of rainbow trout from the lake.

Rose was doing the dishes and humming a song back in the kitchen. Our five children were all married and gone and it was just the two of us again.

I refueled the stove with wood and put a tape in our little cassette player. I sat down in front of the open fire and our children began to sing "Precious Mem'ries."

I listened, leaning way back in my chair, soaking up the heat and watching as the flames from each stick joined together and disappeared up the chimney. This old log building has such a warmth and quietness about it on such a cold winter night. What a difference from the land where corn and cotton grew in Texas where I was raised. It seemed so long ago when as a boy of sixteen, I had driven a truck with a Combine loaded on it all the way from Van Alstyne, Texas to Northern Alberta, Canada when my folks decided to move. This was a nine day trip made in 1957. What an awful loss when our house went up in smoke that winter. Then I met and married a Canadian pioneer girl and we had five wonderful children born to us. Always wanting to be a food producer, I filed on 320 acres that was totally covered with trees. After thirty four years of hard work for me and my family, the Bank got our land and we had to move out of the log home we had built in 1970 to retire in. But, the sun comes up just the same.

I let my thoughts carry me back to when I was a three year old boy living on a farm about fifty miles north of Dallas, Texas. The year was 1943. My Mom and Dad were trying to make a living with agriculture, using mules to do the farm work.

It was a beautiful morning with not a cloud in the sky. The hot days of summer were cooling off now. Mother called "Breakfast" and my brother Blue and I jumped out of bed and dressed fast.

We could smell the home cured ham cooking and we knew there would be fresh biscuits, eggs and white gravy to go with it. We never wanted to miss breakfast.

At the breakfast table the plans for the day were laid out. At that time there was a crew of four, Daddy, Mother, Blue and me.

"Blue" was really my older brother's nick name, given to him as a baby as he was always dressed in blue. From that time on, he has been Blue.

Wanted! Lisa, Manny, Annabelle, Stan, Rose, Jerry and Darla

Chapter Two
Corn 'n Cotton

My Dad was a share cropper. That meant we lived on someone's farm and farmed it for a share of the crop.

This farm was located about a mile east of Kelly, Texas.

Mom and Dad were poor and they didn't have money for a tractor so most of the farming was done with mules. This meant things didn't get done very fast and the work was hard.

There had been lots of rain making wonderful crops and gardens. Now, the weather had cleared up, the fields had dried so the harvest work could get started.

What a beautiful morning, with the sun already warming the earth and a light breeze blowing. The mocking birds were tuning up and down by the creek, I could hear the old whippoorwill. I could hear a chicken cackling out at the chicken house and I knew there was fresh egg laid.

Today was the day to start gathering corn and that was done by hand. Daddy had the cows milked and the pigs fed while Mother was cooking breakfast.

Usually the first thing in the morning was to get the fire going in the cook stove, as it took a while to get it hot enough to cook on.

We had running water, that is you had to run and get it if it hadn't rained for a while and the cistern was dry. The cistern was a big tank above ground that held rain water. It was filled with a pipe running from the eavestrough to the cistern.

Of course all this getting ready to start gathering corn meant we had to get started early. Well, Mother washed the dishes and did a little house cleaning. She split some wood for the noon fire and carried some water into the house so when she got home, she would be ready to cook dinner.

She was part of the corn gathering crew, which meant she had to be ready to go when the mules and wagon came up to the house.

Daddy went off to the barn to catch the mules and harness them up to pull the wagon that the corn was to be loaded into. As we had no tractor for these jobs, the mules had to do.

Blue and I had to go along and help our Dad catch the mules, as we were part of the "crew." He was about five and I was three.

When we got to the barn one mule was easy to catch. My Dad put the bridle and harness on him and he was ready. Blue held him while Daddy went to get the other one.

Well, he was a different mule and had no intention of being caught and having a harness put on him. He stood with his hind end sticking out of the barn door. When my Dad got close to him, both back feet came flying out at him. This went on for a while then my Dad picked up a long pole, reached over and touched the mule's rear. The mule kicked, he touched him again, the mule kicked again.

It seemed like about an hour of this and then the mule turned around and stuck his head out of the door as if to say, "You win, put the bridle on me, I'm ready now."

The mules were hooked up and Blue and I crawled into the wagon box. It looked like a pretty big box to fill with corn.

When we got to the house, Mother was ready to go. Daddy took her hand and helped her up into the wagon and told her, "Step fast, these mules are ready to go this morning!"

Mother had a strange looking thing she'd carried from the house and brought it up into the wagon with her. It looked all wet. I asked her what that thing was. She said, "Well, when we get thirsty, we can get a drink of water out of it and it will be nice and cool. This is a gallon jug with a sack wrapped around it several times. I took some thread and sewed it together so it will stay in place and then I poured water all over it so it will stay cool." It wasn't long until both Blue and I had to try it out, we got awful thirsty and it sure was nice and cool.

We weren't long getting down to the corn field. The wagon had no springs and had iron wheels so it was rough and noisy. For doing this kind of job, two mules were all that were needed as they could pull a full load with no problem.

When we drove into the corn field, the mules had to walk between a row of corn and there were two rows between them. They were supposed to walk along slowly.

Mother was on one side of the wagon walking along between two rows and tearing the ears of corn off the stalks as she went and throwing them into the wagon.

One side of the box had an extension on it called the "throw board" so the ear of corn could hit it and fall down into the wagon. That way the person didn't have to watch so close when they threw the ear of corn.

Daddy tied the long leather lines that came from the mules bridles onto the front of the box that Blue and I were in. Then he told us to try and not get hit by the ears of corn flying into the box.

He was going to be behind the wagon, tearing off the corn from the stalks as they came out behind the wagon as the two rows between the mules went under the wagon. Those stalks were badly bent over and the person behind the wagon had to work fast so he didn't get so far behind that he couldn't throw his ear of corn into the box. Sometimes an ear of corn would get knocked off the stalk with the wagon going over it, so the one gathering the "down rows" had to pick them up as well.

Everything went fine for a while. My brother and I had ring side seats of all this action. Once the box got half full I could even see over the side what was going on.

My Mother and Dad were really working fast. I thought it was kind of neat. There was always one or two ears in the air at the same time! Sometimes if we forgot to watch, we would get hit.

We helped a little by moving the corn to the front so the box would be full and we had a higher place to stand.

All of a sudden, both mules jumped and took off as hard as they could go. I looked back just in time to see my Dad's hands grab onto the back of the wagon and in he came!

By the time he got to the front of the wagon and a hold of the lines, we were really moving. Corn was flying off the stalks from the mules' legs and from the wagon and going higher in the air than the wagon.

Well, when mules decide to run because something has spooked them you really can go for a ride. We made a big circle in the field and when the mules started to get tired of pulling this wagon half full of corn as fast as they could, Daddy drove them back to where this race had started.

He pulled on the lines and asked them to walk and they gladly did. He got out of the back of the wagon and carried on where he had left off.

5

When the wagon was full, Mother and Daddy both climbed in and we started off for home.

At home, while Mom went in to cook dinner, us men went on to the barn. Daddy parked the wagon close to the corn crib where he unhooked the mules from the wagon. Then he gave them feed and water. Next, he climbed into the wagon with a big shovel and unloaded it into the corn crib where it would be fed to the cattle, mules, goats and pigs in the winter.

By that time it was time for a race to the house to see what mother had cooked for dinner. After dinner, it was back to the field for more corn until it rained or the field was finished. This was the program for the next few weeks.

Cotton picking time was a similar program. Blue and I had a lot of time to play because the wagon was parked in the field.

Mother and Daddy would each take a "pick sack" as they called it. It was a long sack with a strap on it that they put their head through and the mouth of the sack hung down on one side.

They picked the cotton and stuffed it in the sack until it was full. Then they dragged or carried it back and dumped it into the wagon.

Well, Blue and I could walk along and talk to them while they picked or stay at the wagon. As boys there is always lots of questions on your mind, so we mostly talked and asked questions while they picked.

One morning when it was nice and clear my parents decided it was time to go to town and get some groceries. I didn't see where we needed any groceries. Mother had all the jars full of all kinds of vegetables, wild berries and what was left over from the pork butchering that wasn't salted or put in a brine to cure. Anyway a trip to town sounded great to me!

Daddy finally got the old truck going and away we went to town. It seemed we were going pretty fast but every time we turned a corner, I would look back and see our old dog coming. He got to town almost as soon as we did.

With the groceries bought, a big ice cream cone that cost five cents and the dog in the truck, we headed for home.

Mother started talking about this goat that we had and how much mischief it had been getting into lately. She suggested Daddy should do something about it.

Well, it sounded like bad news to Blue and me, because that goat was kind of the center of attraction. It would always climb up on the wood pile or the shop roof and watch and see if we could too.

When we got home there was real entertainment for us. The goat had climbed on top of the water cistern, jumped through the window and gotten into Mother's clothes closet. It had eaten some of her clothes and part of her nice straw hat.

Well, that was the end of our entertainment. He became food for the table and there was no question of the matter.

Keith & Louise Hale and their children, in Worsley Baptist Church, 1993 (from L to R) Jerry, Blue, K, Keith, Louise, Dick, Charlotte and Jody

Jerry Hale, June 22, 1994

Chapter Three
The Good Old Days

I can remember one cold day. Mother helped me get on a warm coat and cap, then she said, "You have to go to the field, find your Dad and tell him to come home right away. It is time for your little brother to be born. Hurry!"

So off I went across the yard. I could hear the tractor so I knew where he was. My Dad's brother had a tractor that he let my Dad use when he wasn't using it. I found him and he carried me home.

He was in a big hurry. He took Blue and me to our Grandma's place for the night. Then he took another woman and hurried back home.

The next morning he came and got us and when we got home here was a new brother. I looked at him and thought, "Well, our goat is gone, now we have a new little brother to play with, that's O.K."

Mother said, "His name is Joseph Edward." I thought, "What a big name for such a little baby, Blue is bigger than him and his name is only Blue."

Time went fast and we were getting big now. We had an old Ram sheep that was getting pretty mean and our Dad said, "Boys, today is the day to show the old Ram who's boss. He's been scaring you boys long enough. Both of you take a good stick and go down and give him a good licking."

Well, we felt pretty big. This was our big chance, take on the old Ram as a team and this was going to be fun! The old boy didn't make us look too long for him, he met us at the gate.

Since we both had a big stick he backed away from the gate far enough for us to enter, then he nailed me right in the belly and down I went. My defense weapon went flying and Blue didn't know just what he should do. I decided to get up and do what we had come to do but before I got back on my feet, Wham again and down I went. The old boy just backed up and dared me to get up again. But after two hard slams I thought it best to lie there. I told Blue, "Go and get Daddy, he's big and he can get him off me." Someday, I'd get big enough to try him again.

One night I was awakened out of a sound sleep. Dogs were barking and it wasn't our dog! There were several dogs barking, pigs squealing and calves bawling. It was dark outside.

I heard my Dad get up and he was getting dressed in a hurry. Blue and I jumped out of bed, got dressed and took off after Daddy.

He had a light and was running toward the barn where all the noise was coming from. He picked up a stick and jumped over the fence yelling and swinging the stick. He was knocking dogs a flying.

There was a bunch of dogs in with the pigs and calves. They'd already killed several and were ripping and tearing at the rest. It was a horrible sight!

I realized at my early age that all people are not the same. We went to see one of our neighbors after it got daylight to tell him their dog was part of the pack. The dog came around the corner of the house just then, his whole head was covered with blood. The man said, "My dog would never do anything like that, he's been here all night. You must be mistaken." Then he just turned and went back into the house.

Early one morning, Blue came running into the house all exited and hollering, "The pickup tires are all gone!" It was that period of time in the "forties" when tires were hard to find and someone had come in the night and taken all the wheels off the old pickup and left it sitting on the ground. We had no pickup to use for quite some time. We finally got more tires for the pickup.

One day my Grandpa was at our place and my Dad was trying to get the old pickup going. My Dad was a wonderful man, but he did have a little bit of a hot temper.

This day the old pickup was getting to him. I guess when you grew up working with mules and horses and had to start learning machines and motors, it had to be kind of difficult.

Anyway, they finally decided to give the old truck a pull to start it. Well, it back-fired and caught fire. Everything stopped; Daddy came barreling out of the truck and over to the side of the road where there was a little dirt. He started scraping dirt up with his hands and throwing it onto the fire.

His Dad looked at him quite calmly, and said, "Son, what are you doing? I thought you said you wished it would catch fire and burn up." After that statement he helped Daddy put the fire out. They finally managed to get the truck started and all was well.

One time one of our milk cows had gone through a barbed wire fence and cut her udder pretty bad. Mother milked the cows quite often but this wasn't working well, milking the cow with such bad cuts.

So they decided they'd have to throw the cow down to doctor her and possibly put in some stitches. Well, after quite some time, the cow was on the ground, Mother was holding her head down and Daddy was the Doctor.

The old cow decided that she'd had enough of that and gave a big swing with her head and one of her horns stuck into Mother's leg just below the knee. Well, her holding the cow down was over and the cow had to heal up on her own. Mother hopped around for a while with one bad leg, but in time it got all right.

One day it came time to sell some pigs. If you have never tried loading pigs without a good chute, you have missed an experience. We didn't have a good chute.

Daddy had put some bales of hay on the ground behind the pickup and the pigs had to climb up on the bales and into the truck.

One was a big Sow (mother pig) and was just about loaded when she decided to change direction. So right over the top of Mother she went, knocking her down. When Mother tried to get up she said, "I can't get up, my hip is out of place!"

After about a month of dragging one leg around, it was time to load pigs again. Almost the same performance took place and down she went again. Then she hollered, "My hip is back in place!" The pigs got loaded and off to town they went.

After breakfast one day, Daddy said, "Today is the day the mule is going to get rode. I need one of those mules broke so I can ride him sometimes."

A mule is a cross between a donkey and a horse. They are pretty tough and have a lot of endurance.

After catching "Jack" and putting a saddle on him, we took him out in the yard where there was lots of room to practice. Daddy got on and was ready for a real ride, which he was about to get!

This mule thought it was all right for a harness to be put on to pull a wagon; but to have a saddle strapped on, then a guy climbs on too, that was something he had no intention of putting up with. He thought the only way to resolve this was to try to send him flying.

We had a big wood pile close by which he went right over top of bucking, kicking and doing all he could to get rid of his passenger. He would go up in the air, both back feet would fly backwards in the air, feet would go left, up again, and feet fly out to the side.

We had a wind charger that was built up on a platform about twenty feet high. The wind charger was a generator with a propeller on it that when the wind blew, it turned the generator and charged the batteries so we had electric lights.

My brothers and I were getting a real show with ringside seats at no cost! Ol' Jack got real close to the wind charger and this time he went so high in the air that as a boy, it looked like he went as high as the charger. We were sure proud of our Dad, we thought he had to be the best bronco rider in the world!

One of the neighbor boys wanted to buy a horse from my Dad one day. Frances didn't have any money but he sure wanted this nice horse. That was about the only mode of transportation young guys had and it was a big necessity.

So Daddy sold him the horse to be paid for at a dollar a month. It wasn't long until we heard there had been a bad accident.

A bunch of boys were riding and decided to change horses without getting off. Frances jumped but fell between the horses. His newly purchased horse jumped and kicked. A hind hoof caught him in the side of his forehead, caving his head in.

He had a long ride in a wagon pulled by mules to get to a hospital. He was unconscious for a long time but he lived to tell the story. After he came to, my Dad marked his bill "paid in full."

With people needing horses and mules every day, there were always lots of incidents. One day, one of my uncles hooked up a team of mules to go get a load of coal for the winter.

On his way home with a big load of coal, he had to climb a steep hill. One of the mules, which he'd gotten as a wedding present from his father in law, had a reputation of being balky and when he got tired or decided he wanted a rest, he stopped for a rest, it didn't matter to him where or when. So on this hill, with a load of coal, was where he stopped to rest. It was getting late in the day.

My uncle, Spencer was a very patient man but after trying everything and every way he knew to get him moving and finding that nothing worked, he remembered one old trick that some people had used and decided to give it a try.

So he went off to the side of the road, got an armful of wood and lit a fire under him. This had to be a sure way of action. It wasn't long until the fire was going good and sure enough, it worked! The mule decided to move on, but just far enough to get the wagon on top of the fire and it was time for another rest. Well, there sure was a busy man for a while trying to get the fire out from under the wagon before it caught fire. The wagon was unhooked and left there for the next day.

There were always new stories about someone that had bought their first automobile after driving mules and horses. There was many a wreck as people would get excited and in a tight spot and start yelling, "Whoa," and pulling back on the steering wheel and it still wouldn't stop. Things got bent and broken and sometimes smashed up pretty badly.

In the summer, it was always a boy's delight to hear there was going to be a family get-together on Sunday somewhere. That meant there was sure to be lots of ice-cream. Most people had at least one milk cow which meant there was milk for ice-cream. There would be at least four different kinds made to sample.

After it was mixed up, it was put into gallon freezers. Then the freezers would go into larger wooden containers, which were then filled all around with pieces of ice. Salt would then be added on the top to make the frost go inside. Then an old blanket was placed on top of that. Usually a small boy sat on the blanket to hold everything down and keep it from turning over, while a bigger boy or man got a hold of the crank and started turning.

After about twenty minutes, it would start to get hard to turn and you knew it was ready. If you forgot to check the hole where the salty water was supposed to drain out as the ice melted and a piece of ice happened to plug the hole, it was a terrible disappointment to take the cover off and upon sampling, find that salt had gotten into the ice cream and all this time and work was for nothing and you would have to start all over again. You learned to keep a watchful eye on the little hole after that to make sure it didn't get plugged up.

Mother's Day was always a special time to me. On Mother's Day, there were always lots of flowers growing and on that day, everyone took fresh flowers to the cemetery where their family was buried. After all the flowers were put on, it looked real nice.

There were always some graves that had no flowers on them, so I would watch and find some graves that had lots of flowers on them and when no one was watching, I'd borrow a few and go around and put some on them. "There," I thought, "that looks better." That

12

was always a special day.

After all the ice cream, playing with cousins, and the special time at the cemetery, we were all kind of anxious to get to bed because all week we had been busy packing and loading, getting ready for the big move.

Our home beside the Tatogga Lake

Murray Wood, Jerry & Rose Hale, Bruce & Charlotte Parker

Chapter 4
A Place Of Our Own

"Get up, boys, breakfast is ready and we've got a big day ahead of us!" We knew what this meant. We had been renting land up until now, had bought our own place and it was time to get moving. After the table grace, breakfast and Daddy had read from the Bible, we were ready.

We had made a few trips already so I knew the road, but today was going to be different; I was going to ride a horse and follow my Dad with his tractor and wagon loaded with our belongings.

I had to have a hand to get up on the horse as a boy of seven doesn't have very long legs. The horse really didn't want to leave the old place so it took me for a little circle around the yard, around the little shop, under a tree and since the big limbs were level with the horse's back, he ducked his head and I went sliding off and onto the ground. I looked up and wondered how it could happen so fast!

Daddy had a change of plans since this wasn't going to work. He would tie the horse to the back of the wagon and lead it. That worked good for a while, then the horse decided to stop and broke the board on the wagon it was tied to.

"Well, Jerry, ridin' time again," so up on the horse I went again. The farther we went the slower the horse wanted to go. It was a ten mile trip and about half way there we came to a farm that had a bunch of mules. My horse decided to turn in there to check out these mules and I couldn't do anything about that choice.

When we went in around the house there was a lady washing clothes in a big round pot with a fire under it. She had a stick pushing the clothes down in the water. She realized I had a problem and came over with her stick and gave it to me. Man, did we take off.

It wasn't long until I caught up with my Dad. We got to this new place just before dark. It wasn't much of a place but it was going to be home for a few years. Mother and my three brothers were there with supper for us. Dudley K was the newest playmate of the family.

We had all just lain down and weren't asleep yet when we heard our dog coming with some hounds after him. There was no door on the room we were sleeping in. It was warm and it didn't make any difference without a door, the whole house was in about the same shape.

Well, the hounds got closer and closer, then around the house they came. On the second trip around our dog noticed an opening, so in he come and right under Mother and Daddy's bed, hounds right behind!

Daddy raised up in bed and let out a yell you could have heard for miles. Now this was something new for the hounds to find this place was suddenly occupied with something with a loud voice.

They all hit the opening in retreat at the same time. You would have thought there was a raccoon biting on each hound's ear, the bawling they were doing trying to get out of there. There must have been a dozen of them.

Our dog's name was Vic and old Vic never moved from under that bed all night. That was the safest place he'd found in a long time.

The old house was full of rats and mice. The rats had long tails. They played tag and relay races all night. War was declared on all these unwelcome residents and we boys had lots of fun.

It was on this farm that a sister, Charlotte and another brother, Dick Don was born making five boys and one girl in the family.

"We got to clean this place up so we can grow cotton and corn and maybe have some cattle here, boys," Daddy told us after breakfast one day.

I looked out the window and it looked like the grass had not been mowed for at least ten years and beyond that there were sunflowers so thick you couldn't see through them. It looked as though they were at least ten feet tall and they were good for nothing except to create work!

I knew by Daddy's announcement that there was not going to be much idle time for the Hale boys. But amongst the work we found some time to play.

We had two horses now. One day we decided to make a cart and hook it up to one of the horses.

Since Blue was older he was full of lots of good ideas. He decided I should ride one horse alongside the horse pulling the cart and that Jody (which had become Joseph's nickname) should ride Chester, the one with the harness on and pulling the cart, because Jody could hang on to the harness. We didn't have saddles so something to hang on to meant you could ride and stay on a horse through anything. Blue was going to ride on this homemade contraption and drive Chester.

It was a beautiful day. Mother was working in the garden so we had to get around on the other side of the house while we were getting all rigged up, because if she would have seen what we were doing she would have stopped us, because somebody might get hurt.

Well, we got all hooked up and ready to roll. Jody was on Chester, Blue was in the driver's position and I was on the other horse beside and off we went. Mother hadn't suspected a thing.

We didn't go many feet with the iron wheels rattling on the gravel road when Chester didn't like all this noise and thought the best thing to do was get away from it. So he was at a dead run real quick but this noisy contraption stayed right behind him. Next he decided maybe his back feet would get rid of it and his first smashing blow to the front of this rig sent a bunch of boards and the master driver, Blue, flying through the air.

Blue skidded to a stop on the gravel, which is kind of hard on a boy's skin. We never wore shirts; they took too much time getting on and off.

By this time Mother had picked up on all this noise and came running around the house and down the road. She thought she could stop this wild episode.

After getting rid of Blue off the cart, Chester kept at full speed but it still took a lot of kicking to get rid of wheels and all the boards. After a half mile down the road he made a circle in a neighbor's yard and there the wheels and most of the boards came off. Jody was still in top place hanging onto the hames and having a free ride.

The horse had no intention of stopping for Mother. He made a right turn then headed for a creek bottom about a mile and a half away that was growing corn.

When a horse is scared, the other one has to be pretty mad to catch him; and the horse I was riding wasn't as mad as Chester was scared, so I wasn't having much luck catching him.

Mother was coming behind us now as fast as she could run, crying and yelling, "Catch him! Catch him!" I was going at full speed and riding with no saddle. When we got to the place where we normally turned into the pasture, my horse turned, but I went straight ahead. When I jumped up and looked, Chester was going over the horizon with Jody sitting high on the throne.

I had to get my horse caught again, lead it over to a fence post, climb up on the post then on the horse. Away we went again.

I caught up with them in the corn field. The horse had run until he got tired and stopped. Jody was crying. He didn't know how he was going to get home!

We met Mother and Blue about half way back and that was quite a reunion. We must have been quite a rough looking bunch. Blue left some skin on the gravel road and had some signs of blood and dirt mixed. I had leveled off some of the dirt road with my face. Mother was almost exhausted from running. Jody was in great shape still hanging onto the harness.

Mother didn't know if she should be mad at us or happy we were still alive. Mothers raising a bunch of boys have to be cheered for; they are put through some tough spots.

Needless to say we didn't try that again, but there were many other things we had to check out.

My Dad had bought a corn sheller and was buying corn from the neighbors. They would bring their wagon load of corn and my Dad would buy it. The wagon was unloaded by hand into the sheller that would separate and put the shucks in a pile. In the winter we baled the shucks and they became cow feed. The cobs were put in another pile and the kernels went into a truck to be sold.

It was a Saturday afternoon and the men that worked there had gone home for the weekend. There were still a half a dozen wagons full, so Daddy, Blue and I were going to finish off emptying the wagons so that Monday morning, the farmers could get their wagons and gather some more corn.

Things seemed to be going all right until about the third load. Then the old tractor that drove the sheller with a long belt and had the exhaust stack sticking straight out, blew a spark into the fine dust and immediately a fire was going!

When Blue and I saw it we thought the safest place to be was away from there, so we jumped out of the wagon and were on a dead run for home. Daddy looked around for us and we were gone. He ran us down and told us to get back and help him. He very quickly outlined what we had to do while we were running back.

By the time we got back, the tractor, a 2236 IHC, was on fire and the fire was spreading fast. Daddy jumped on the old tractor and backed it out where there was some dirt. I expected the gas tank to blow at anytime. He got the fire put out with dirt.

By this time Blue and I had moved all the neighbor's tractors and wagons and the grain truck out to safety. The sheller got burned some, but we got it out to safety and the fire was put out.

There were a lot of events that went with the corn sheller days. The tractor power for driving these machines was old, so for a safety measure and to have a spare, my Dad went to check out another tractor, the same as we had, a 2236 IHC.

Those were the days before electric starters were installed on machinery. There was a crank out the front that you had to turn the motor over with to start the motor. On the magneto side, there was a little lever that you were supposed to turn down to retard the spark. This would prevent the engine from firing too soon and backfiring and kicking the handle out of your hand.

Well, when my Dad was checking the compression on this other tractor, he forgot to turn the lever down. He had to turn the crank part way and it fired, kicked the handle backward and jerked it from his hand. It hit him on the forearm and broke it. His hand just fell over backwards.

That was pretty tough for him for a while because everything required a lot of manual labor. But it wasn't long until he had the cast off and was going again with two arms. He thought a tractor with that much compression had to be good, so he bought it and we had a spare.

We needed to build a shed to store whole corn in so it could be ground in the winter to feed to the cattle. Daddy had some men helping him build this shed and they were putting tin on the roof one day when it came time for me to get the milk cow in and milk her. I had to go by this shed and someone yelled something.

I looked up and here came a sheet of tin heading right for me. The wind had blown it out of his hand. I jumped sideways but not enough and it caught me on the calf of my leg cutting it to the bone.

After a few days in the hospital having about one hundred and twenty little muscles stitched together, the skin the shape of a horse shoe stitched in place and a cast on, I was ready to go home.

It didn't seem too bad, people would bring me things, I didn't have to milk or do anything, I thought it was kind of like being a King. People visited me and some would leave me twenty cents, some fifty cents and a few even gave me a dollar. The day I got my cast off was a great day but I still couldn't get around very good. I now had twelve dollars of my very own; that was a huge amount to me.

Chapter 5

Early Lessons

Mother was going for groceries and I got permission to go with her to the store. Well, I spotted this wrist watch and it had a price tag of twelve dollars on it. I had never had a watch and I thought, "This is just what I need."

I thought about it and looked at it several times thinking, "Now, I have twelve dollars, if I give it all, I won't have any to put in the offering at Church tomorrow." My Sunday School Teacher had said that a tenth of what we have belongs to God and I had a terrible time deciding. After about a half hour of agony, because for a twelve year old boy that was a tough decision, I decided I'd put in one dollar and twenty cents in the offering tomorrow. I remembered my Teacher had said to bring your tithes and offerings into the store-house.

By and by maybe someone else might give me enough to buy the watch, so I left it and it was time to go home. I felt like a huge decision had been made.

The evening chores were done, supper over and a pickup drove into our yard. The man that owned the store got out of the truck and he had a little box in his hand. He gave it to me and said, "Everyone your age needs one of these." I opened it and there was the watch I had been looking at and dreaming about. I just about cried, I was so happy! I knew boys that big weren't supposed to cry, but I did a little anyway. I never forgot the lesson I learned there.

It was a late Saturday when we got word that we needed to go to town, because a train had run into one of our horses. We got there and sure enough it was my Dad's horse.

At that time, we had some Spanish people working for us in the winter to help care for the cattle. One of them decided he needed some alcohol, so he took Daddy's horse and went into town. He got to drinking and forgot about the horse. The horse decided to go home and had to cross the railroad tracks. A train had come and knocked it down and cut off all it's legs just below the knee. It wrecked the saddle too.

We had the vet come and put the horse to sleep. That was a bad day for me; I had trouble sleeping. I dreamed of this every night for a long time.

I remember when we received word that one of my uncles had a wreck and had almost cut his scalp off. He was very drunk.

As a young inquisitive boy, I wondered why people would do these foolish things, but no one could give me a good reason for doing them. Later on, I found out that we humans don't always do things for good reasons, sometimes we just do them and later we wonder why.

Our dog, Vic was a real family friend. We had lots of snakes around home and some were poisonous. Ol' Vic was always watching out for us and killed lots of snakes.

Sometimes we took a big chance when we went to get the eggs after dark. Some snakes, especially copperheads or chicken snakes would get in the chicken nests and eat the eggs and if it happened to be lunch time for him when you stuck your hand in for eggs, it was a terrible surprise.

I'm sure Ol' Vic kept us from snake bites. Sometimes I'd look at him after he'd had a bout with a snake and his head would be swollen twice its normal size and I'd wonder, "Well, Ol' boy, are you going to come out of this one?" He was always a faithful friend. When his eyesight failed and he was run over by a car, his funeral was kind of hard.

The summers were always really hot, especially when it came time to hoe corn and it was taller than your head and no wind and a hot sun.

We had to go between the rows and cut out everything that wasn't corn. Riding a tractor with iron seats got really hot when we were working. When we stopped for lunch and came back I'm sure you could have fried an egg on that seat!

But that hot weather was sure a good time to kill weeds. It is no wonder that kind of work is non existent anymore. There was no part of it that was fun except the last two minutes of the day's work.

I recall a special day for me. One of my older cousins that was married and had three girls and a little boy still in diapers, came to get me!

We went on a week's vacation in their Army Jeep pulling a little trailer behind. They had food and all the camping gear needed to stop and camp for the night. With seven of us in the little Jeep, we had real togetherness.

At night everyone had their little chores to do to help around camp. I felt like an honored king for them to have made a place for me in the Jeep. For a thirteen year old boy, it was a memory that would last a lifetime.

Most of the summer we moved our beds out in the yard to sleep. We had no air conditioning in those days and one hundred and ten degrees made the house awfully hot. We always had to be mindful of our beds outside when it looked like rain. Sometimes we would wake up at night with so much thunder, lightning and rain in our faces, there was nothing to do but jump up, grab our clothes and bedding and hit for the house to finish the night inside!

There were lots of tornadoes and most people had what they called a "storm cellar." It was made of cement or a huge culvert. It was also a good place to store vegetables and all the summer's canning, as there were no deep freezers.

These storm cellars were underground so sometimes if it seemed like the storm was going to be a bad one, everyone got out of bed and into the storm cellar. What a long night that always was!

One uncle and aunt who lived in town, heard a storm coming and decided it was time to get out of the house. They started running for their car just as the wind hit. Before they got to the car, a flying two by four went tearing through my uncle's leg. If they would have stayed in the house they would have been gone. Their house was gone, several blocks away!

Chapter 6
School Fun

One morning one of my friends was walking from home to catch the school bus and had to cross a bridge. Well, on this bridge was a skunk. My friend, Odis kicked the skunk off the bridge, caught the bus and went on to school.

After school had been going for about an hour, the smell of skunk was getting very high in the school and the principal decided us boys should go look for the skunk.

It took us a couple of hours to check under and around the school looking for this skunk. Finally one of the girls decided she was going to get sick if the skunk smell wasn't removed. She told the teacher that Odis had kicked the skunk off the bridge and of course you can't do that without getting strong perfume on your pants.

Well, our fun was over, we had to go back to work and Odis had to walk home. But the smell lingered pretty strongly in the school for several days.

I've seen my dog get sprayed in the face by a skunk sometimes when I was trapping. He would get so sick he would put his head on the ground to try and rub it off; but it is not easily removed.

One of the ways I got a few pennies for spending money was to sell skunk and opossum pelts. At night was the best time to hunt them with a dog, a flashlight and a 22 because at night they would be in the persimmon trees.

One night I shot a nice 'possum and cleaned it up nice and told my Dad, "I think it would be good to eat." Some people did eat them.

Well, he looked at it and agreed he thought it would be good if Mother would cook it. Dad and I never found anything we couldn't eat. Mother agreed and baked it up nice with potatoes and at supper time it looked like a real delicacy. Mother had cooked some other meat for the rest of the family because they were all sure that this special dish would not be good.

My Dad cut off a nice piece of meat and because I always liked the liver that was my first choice. Well, Daddy started chewing on his meat and I started on the liver. I kind of watched him from the corner of my eye. I could see he was chewing and chewing but not swallowing.

After a while he took the meat out of his mouth, wrapped it in a napkin and I thought, "Well, if he can't, I can't either," so I did likewise. Needless to say we never bothered Mother any more to cook us any more 'possum.

Being farm boys going to school, we often had a cow to milk before we caught the school bus. When we got home from school and had a snack, we had to be outside helping our Dad with whatever needed doing some of us farm boys looked at the kids that lived in town and how after school they would get to play around the school and have all kinds of fun, while we had to go home and get to work helping Mother and Daddy.

The farm children were really a big asset to their parents especially after they got big enough to help do things not just get in the way. So, we made a plan one day.

We decided if it came time for us to catch the bus for home, if the bus had no keys in it, that would mean we would get to stay and play for a while at the school like the other kids. So at noon hour we had to find our bus. Sure enough, the keys were in it. It was indeed our lucky day!

The bus driver also had a small place where he sold hamburgers. You could get a hamburger for fifteen cents, a Coke for five cents and a candy bar for five cents, so for a quarter you could get a pretty good meal.

Well, I don't know who was watching our performance, but when we thought we had everything planned out well and everything going according to plan, the principal came into our classroom, pointed his finger and said, "You, You, You and You come with me."

So we followed him out kind of sheepishly. We still didn't know what really was up but he led us to his car and said, "Get in, boys, we're going for a little ride."

When we got to the bus, he said "Boys, where are the keys?" Well, we knew we'd been seen by someone and there was no way out. The grass was tall where we had thrown the keys and it took quite a bit of looking before we found them.

Back in the principal's office, we found out crime doesn't pay. One at a time we had to take our position in front of a wooden paddle, with ten swats on the rear delivered by none other than the principal.

Between my school teachers, principals and my Dad, I was one of those boys that was raised with a board and I was raised quite frequently.

Looking back at that style, type and method of punishment, it sure caused me to respect and appreciate authority; contrary to what some folks believe today. Needless to say, we never tried that key plan anymore, it was abandoned.

Rose and her daughters, Annabelle, Lisa and Darla in front of Tatogga Lake Resort

Jerry, Rose and Manny at their first home in Worsley, Ab., 1961

Chapter 7
Blue and I

We had a brand new swimming pool and our neighbors had one too. They were full of water and it was time to try them out.

It was a beautiful, sunny Sunday afternoon. Blue and I were out riding our horses with our neighbor boys that had their new pool built at the same time.

We decided the temperature was just right so we hit their pool first. We swam for a while, then decided to go try ours.

Robbie and I went first. We stuffed our clothes under our arms, climbed on our horses and away we went. We rode out through the gate and up the road; there was a fence on both sides.

We rode the half mile and into the gate that was the entrance to the new swimming pool we were heading for. The pool was a big hole made with a bull dozer.

As we went through the gate we saw a car coming. We looked back and saw that Blue and Ken were on the road about half way between the gates. The car had a neighbor woman and her daughter in it.

Robbie and I knew the boys were in a real jam. They had no place to go and nowhere to hide; because in those days, we never had swim suits. They had just tucked their pants under their arm, jumped on their horses and headed for the second pool.

What a spot to be caught in. We learned to be a lot more careful after that!

For Christmas one year, my Dad bought his Dad a box of little Melba cigars. Blue and I kept looking at them and thinking, if

Grandpa smokes them, they must be really good. So, after much persistence, one night Daddy said, "Well, boys, I guess the time has come since you're all grown up now and wanting to try a man's smoke, that you are going to get the chance."

He went to the box and took out two cigars, gave them to us, lit a match for us and we were on our way. We felt pretty big and bold. Of course to be like a man you have to inhale.

Well, after about a quarter was gone I started feeling kind of funny. This wasn't quite like it was when I started. Pretty soon Blue started looking funny, the lights started to spin.

Grandpa never said anything like this ever happened to him. I had to butt mine out and Blue did too. We were two very sick boys and after losing our suppers, we didn't have the strength to make it to bed.

So Daddy felt sorry for his two young men and carried us off to bed, what a wonderful place. We were cured of cigars from Grandpa's box.

I guess all brothers are not the same and there are a lot of different opinions today on child behavior. Blue and I were always close in everything, but we had a lot of fights over almost anything. Of course he being older and the instigator most of the time, it was his fault.

We each had a cow to milk and were doing quite well with about a half a gallon in each pail when he decided to put a little excitement into this boring job one evening. So he turned one teat towards me and gave me the whole shot. Then of course, it had to be my turn. This didn't last long until we left the pail of milk sitting right there and we were behind the cows seeing who could get the evening blow.

Jody decided he needed some help to stop this and away he went to the house to get Mother to come to the rescue. We were just about ready for a rest when she got to the barn, so it wasn't hard to convince us to stop and carry on with what we were supposed to be doing.

Amazing enough our pails were still upright where we'd left them. She stood around for a few minutes, then said she had to finish supper and for us to come for supper as soon as we had finished.

When we heard the screen door shut on the house, that meant she was back inside and Blue thought I needed one more shot and I got it. That meant he needed one too and the fight was on again.

Jody had to make another trip to the house and here came Mother again. She wasn't very happy this time and two boys went flying.

Then, she sat there until we finished our milking and we all went for supper together.

Mother was usually pretty easy to get along with and most of the time she didn't need any help on the discipline part, but sometimes she would say, "Boys, just wait 'till your Daddy gets home." We knew that meant trouble.

Not to our liking, but most of the time we were privileged to wear overalls that were big enough to wear a couple of years and then pass on down to the next one.

This one day Blue and I had a terrible day and after many fights Mother said, "Boys, just wait 'till your Daddy comes in." We knew what that meant, heat to the seat.

So we decided for our own protection to add a little cushion behind. We were both pretty lean and with the big overalls there was just enough room for a pillow in the rear. We felt we were ready for whatever was coming this time, we could really be tough.

After Daddy had been filled in on the afternoon events, he got a glimpse of the extended size of Blue's overalls in the back and got tickled at the sight. I guess he decided there was no need to reinforce respect for the parents that day, because there was no more mention of it.

One of the unique things was that while we were at home playing or working, Blue and I had lots of fights. But away from home we were best buddies and would fight for each other, so in our case a few bloody noses were just part of growing up.

The type of punishment changed at our place as we grew older, in order to maintain the proper respect necessary. One time my Dad was gone to a cattle sale to buy calves to feed. Mother's parents were visiting with us and one of my brothers got into an argument with Mother. It turned into a scuffle and Mother got her back hurt. I couldn't understand why Mother's Dad never stopped it but he never said a word. With Mother's back hurt, the argument was over. I knew there would be trouble in camp when Dad got home.

Sometime in the middle of the night Dad came up the stairs to where we were sleeping or trying to sleep, and spoke to the one that had the trouble with Mother and said, "Get up and pack your clothes. When a boy gets so big and tough his parents have no control, it's time he gets out. There's a place that can handle boys like you."

It was pretty sad watching my brother pack his clothes to leave and not knowing to where or if I'd ever get to see him again. All kinds of things ran through my mind of the fun we'd had and the bad things we'd done to each other and all the times we'd gone to our grandparent's places together and had wonderful meals, and all the things we had done with our uncles and aunts and cousins and now one brother would be missing all this from now on.

It wasn't long until they left and it was a sad good-bye. In the morning we milked the cows, had breakfast and caught the school bus. It was hard to explain where the other brother was, I just told the bus driver, "He won't be going today."

What a long day that was in school. When we got home I found that my Dad was there and my brother too. My Mother's back was better and I sure was a happy guy.

Blue didn't know that the land taxes were due, but it was a good excuse for my Dad to take Blue on this trip, to where, none of us knew. There was enough time in their travel for him to make all kinds of pleading and promises of good behavior.

Blue had to sit in the pickup in front of the courthouse, while Dad was in paying the taxes. Blue could imagine all kinds of things in his future that were to be totally different from what he had planned. When Dad came out, Blue convinced him to take him back home. That was a lesson that none of us kids ever forgot.

Blue, Jerry, K, Jody and Dick

Chapter 8
Growing Up Fast

Church was part of our weekly events that happened every Sunday, rain or shine. As a boy of twelve years, I asked Jesus to come into my heart and have never been sorry for that choice. I recommend it to everyone.

I had my own horse after raising her and with a little help got her to where I could ride her. I had a special project planned today. A sheep had died in the barn over night and it needed taking out away from there.

I caught my horse and put my saddle on her. I tied a rope to the saddle horn and looped one end around the sheep and away we went. Everything went pretty good. The horse sure didn't like this thing dragging behind her, but we got to where we were going. I got off, took the loop off the sheep and began to roll up the rope. My horse turned, looked at the sheep, let out a snort and decided the best place to be was somewhere else.

The loop caught around my hand and I was on the ground bouncing along like a sled on my stomach. I am sure a horse can run faster when scared than mad and we were moving on. Dirt and grass were hitting me in the face, I couldn't see a thing.

I knew I had to get that rope off my hand and would just about get it, then another bump and it would get pulled tight again. There was no time for calling for help at this speed, I knew nobody would hear me.

I knew we would be coming to a fence and I had closed the gate. I could just see the horse going over the fence and me into the barbed wire. I knew it was going to be a big wreck and there wasn't a thing

I could do.

Several times I just about got the rope off and it would jerk tight again. I knew if I ever needed God's help, it was now and I started asking for it.

About twenty feet from the fence the horse decided to stop and slid right up to it. Then she turned and looked at me, dirty, my clothes half torn off, and leaking a little blood in several places.

She watched me get up and take the rope from my hand as if to say, "How did you like that?" Well, I loved that stop.

I told the Lord I sure appreciated His help in the matter too and I was a lot more careful how I handled a rope after that.

One day Blue and I were at a neighbor's house and it was time to go home. We were riding our horses and Joe said, "I think I'll have you boys a race. I think I can outrun your horses on this gravel road."

We were always game for a race and lined up for the start. Joe hollered, "Go!" and as Blue's horse went past him he grabbed a hold of Chester's tail. Chester probably remembered the incident with the cart behind because we were moving! Joe was covering a lot of ground with each step and a person's legs can only go so fast. He realized he couldn't keep this up much longer so he turned loose and started tumbling in the gravel.

We got our horses stopped and went back. Blue said, "For sure he must be dead, what a mess to be tumbling and sliding in this gravel." Then he told me to go for help.

When I got to the neighbor's house, I was so scared I couldn't say a word. I could only make signs to Joe's uncle and he knew something bad had happened, so he jumped in his truck and drove to where Joe was.

He stopped to check on him then he drove off to get the doctor. We waited until the doctor came. Joe never moved or made a noise; I was sure he was dead. The Doc checked him over and we put him on a bed outside under a big tree, where he stayed for three days and nights. On the fourth day he came to and everything was back to normal.

It always amazed me how some people got picked on by others. Jack was a new boy that moved to our school and it just seemed natural for the other boys to pick on him.

One day our agriculture teacher took my class on a field trip. We rode in the back of his pickup that had stock racks on it, out to a farm. We were going to see some hands-on teaching on pruning trees, dehorning calves and the things he thought farm boys should be taught.

We were in the barnyard and he was teaching us how to castrate pigs. We were in a circle around him watching. Jack was kneeling down close to the teacher trying to watch him, but at the same time watching over his shoulder.

One of the boys was not very interested in what we were being taught but instead, was looking for a chance to do something to Jack. There were a lot of wet corn cobs lying around and this boy picked up one of them and took careful aim to hit Jack when he wasn't looking.

He gave it a hard throw. Jack saw it coming and ducked just in time to miss it. It hit the teacher on the side of his face and put the print of a corn cob on it.

This teacher always did what he called balancing the books every Friday afternoon. That meant during the week if you'd done something bad, he would hold up five or ten fingers; that meant that the punishment would be five or ten licks on the rear with his paddle and would be taken care of on Friday afternoon.

This time with a red print on the side of his head, the rules quickly changed. The pig operation took a halt until after a short court session, a quick verdict and sentence with no chance of an acquittal or postponement or any defense to be heard was completed. He found the closest piece of scrap lumber available. He said, "There's going to be ten for the current event and five for general principals."

So out behind the barn some learning took place that afternoon. After a hot smoking rear-end the boy vowed that he was sorry and he'd try not to do that again. After that matter was taken care of we were back on the pig operation and everyone was paying attention to what was being taught and what we'd learned that day. We learned that sometimes those in authority can change the rules if needed.

There was a neighbor girl down the road I tried to teach how to drive the tractor one day. She ran into the well and smashed part of the wall that was above ground. That was the end of training Loretta. She jumped off the tractor and was on the run for home. It was kind of tough explaining to Daddy that it really wasn't my fault.

Donald Clyde had worked for us for several years. One night in town a guy that was drinking decided he was going to give Donald a licking. I guess he was feeling pretty tough.

Blue and I warned him that there were going to be four in the fight, because we wouldn't allow our friend to be beat up. We weren't very big, but we had already had a lot of fights with each other so we weren't afraid.

Then an older man came by and saw what was about to happen and said, "Mr. Hix, there is going to be five in this here fight because I'm going to help these kids out." That was the end of that.

The school teachers that taught me from grades one through ten all played a big part in shaping my life. They all cared and I knew it.

I got into lots of mischief and most of the time I got caught and it caused some pain at the end of the paddle. My Dad warned me that if I got into trouble at school, I would be in trouble with him.

Blue used this situation to his advantage quite a bit. To keep him from taking home the wrong report of the day, I had to do many favors for him.

One day, my teacher, the principal, told the boys in my class to clean up the gym and when we were finished, there would be a case of pears for us to help ourselves to. A few of us boys had two pears.

Then back in class, the principal called us one by one to the front of the class and gave us each ten licks with his paddle for eating two pears.

If I could relive that time, one principal would remember the day that he was a show-off one too many times, but I didn't want to be in trouble at home too, so I took the licking.

One day Mrs. Jones' class was giving her a hard time and with the doors all open to the hallway, we heard her tell her class, "I'm going to quit. I can't put up with kids like you anymore. I'm finished." She slammed her books on the table and out the door and down the hall she went.

Halfway down the hall she turned around and back she came at a faster pace, into her room, slammed the door, turned up the volume and began.

She said, "I cannot turn you out into the world like this. I'm going to bring you out of it." For the next half hour the rest of the high school learned what her desires and expectations were for her students. I believe because of caring teachers like her, they have helped make the world what it is today.

Chapter Nine
A New Country

Time was moving on and my Dad was tired of cotton and corn. For the past several years he had talked of a place with lots of room to farm and raise cattle. He often talked of a place where he could help start a Church and be self supporting missionary. Almost every summer we took a trip Northwest from Texas but he didn't find what he was looking for.

One day an old friend of the family, Mr.Sherly came for a visit. He recommended that my Dad take a look at the northern part of Alberta, Canada as to him it was a land of opportunity. He said it was a young country with lots of land suitable for farming and lots of timber that would someday provide a lot of jobs. He told us it was a wonderful ranching country and certainly lots of room for more Churches to be built for people to worship the Lord in. Mr.Sherly said to my Dad who was forty five at the time, "Keith, you are getting almost too old, but it will be great for your children".

On one of the trips to the new country, I went with him and I was very impressed at the pioneer way of life that was still lived there. My love for the cotton and corn fields had never been very great and now I had just lost the rest of it. My vote was yes. In this new country when you turned eighteen years old, you could file on 320 acres of land, clear it and it was yours. There were no telephones or T.V. in people's homes and the roads were very poor but my vote was still yes.

On Dad's last searching trip, he bought a half section (320 acres) of land just west of Worsley, Alberta with a little cabin on it. What a place for a young man to dream about.

I had lots of friends here and I knew it would be kind of hard to leave all the things that would be involved in leaving. I had ten years of school here and no idea what lay ahead for me in school from here on. But, Columbus wasn't scared so why should I be? I knew I could make new friends and my list of friends would just be longer.

I had just lost my very best friend. He had gone and gotten married at the ripe old age of eighteen. Since the farm hadn't been sold yet, Blue and his new wife, Betty planned to stay behind and farm it. My Grandpa once said," Tomorrow, everything will be a little different from today". I had to expect the fact that from now on, mine and Blue's lives were going to be different. Blue and Betty agreed to drive a truck loaded with miscellaneous machinery to the new country. I knew this would be a good chance for me to get to know his choice of a life long mate. Our Mom and Dad had tried to share with us as well as be an example of choosing a mate till death do us part.

Word had soon spread that the Hales' were moving North. Some friends were certain to tell us how wrong this was and how foolish we were. Others said, "May God go with you, guide and protect you, we'll be praying for you". I know it was hard for all four of my Grandparents to think of us moving knowing we wouldn't be able to visit much anymore. My Grandparents were all wonderful people and had made a good name for us. They all bade us God's blessings.

We loaded up what we could take on two trucks and sold the rest of our belongings by auction. I guess we were all kind of apprehensive about the moment to leave as our roots ran very deep here. Just before leaving, we formed a circle and my Dad asked the Lord for guidance and safety as we travelled. He also asked for help to remove our roots and plant them in the new country and that God would help us be all He wanted us to be. Amen. No turning back now. So with Blue and Betty in one truck, Mother in the car, Daddy in the pickup pulling a trailer with the Combine header on it, Jerry driving a 1950 ford truck with a Combine on it, we were on our way. Jody, K, Charlotte and Dick took turns riding with who ever they chose for the nine day trip to Worsley, Alberta, Canada. What a caravan!

In 1957 there were few by-passes around the big cities and no radios for communication to keep in touch with each other. It's a wonder we made it as well as we did.

In one of the big cities we had to go through there were two different road signs. There had been a new road built and someone had forgotten to take the old sign down. Blue and I were traveling close together so we both took the same road. When we got outside of town we stopped to make sure Mother and Daddy were with us. Mother wasn't so we waited for a while, then Daddy went back to look for her. When they finally came back there was no peace in the family for a while.

They had eventually gotten the Police involved to find this missing person and found that the two road signs had caused this problem. When it came time to stop for the night, everyone had cooled off and was happy that another day was behind and we were closer to our new home.

Motels were not a part of this trip. We camped out every night. Early one morning, an airplane came over spraying for mosquitoes. We happened to be right in the line of fire. We ended breakfast and broke camp in a hurry that morning. The pilot must have had a good laugh at what he had just sprayed. We must have been a sight worth a good laugh.

After seven days we were at the Canadian border. They told us we were fools for going that far north and that nothing would grow there; but that was our destination.

After finding out that we had to pay eleven hundred dollars to cross the border, we knew if we made it, there wouldn't be much money left when we arrived.

I have sometimes wondered at the decision of some people paying to move in; and yet, others get paid to move in to Canada.

After we passed Edmonton, the roads had gotten progressively worse and the last forty miles had very little if any gravel on the road.

It was August 4, 1957, when we arrived at our new home west of Worsley, Alberta. After a long trip like we had just had with no real serious problems, it truly was a time to give thanks to God for the safety He had granted us.

Our new house wasn't much of a Palace but it was "Home Sweet Home". It was a sixteen by twenty-four foot log dwelling. I'm sure Mother wondered a bit when she thought about the home she'd left behind to move into one with no modern conveniences.

Blue's choice of a mate seemed to be O.K. Betty had a way about her that won all our hearts. It was soon time for them to return to the farm in Texas which would now be their new home. Again we prayed together asking God to give them a safe trip and to be their guide in life. As I bade them farewell and waved them bye there was a big lump in my throat.

As the saying goes, "Home is where the heart is." My heart was here now, the land of many opportunities for a boy of sixteen, with milions of events and opportunities just waiting for me.

It rained day after day. We had trucks to unload and a crop in the field to harvest. Daddy had hired the crop planted in the spring and now it was getting close to harvest. The rain every day really complicated our problems.

One good thing about the rain, it usually kept the water barrel full. It ran from the roof down the eavestroughs and into the barrel.

One of our neighbors had a team of horses hooked to the front of the tractor that was pulling his combine. For people to make a living off the land, they have to be very creative in ideas because each day demands something different.

After the water in the fields turned to ice, we finished our harvest. We had no more problems with getting stuck.

I was very impressed with all the vegetables that this new country produced. The wonderful new friends we had that came and brought vegetables from their gardens impressed me too. Some shared helpful hints and some came to help do what they could to make us feel welcome.

We were truly in a pioneer country with a wonderful bunch of people. They had pioneer spirits of helping, sharing and trying to encourage, because everyone was the same with very little money and all fighting the elements to survive.

There have been a lot of stories told of pioneer men but I want to put a plug here for the pioneer women. They are the ones that had a lot of hardships with no electricity or telephones. Raising a family was lots of work.

Most of them cooked on wood stoves that had to be tended regularly or they would go out. To do their baking, they had to know the right amount of wood to put in for the proper heat. There were no knobs or buttons to set the right temperature.

All water for the household use and washing clothes had to heated on the cook stove. In winter, many homes used melted snow for their water supply. Sometimes in summer, some women had a big pot in the yard over a fire to heat water for washing clothes.

Before the washing machines came along with the gas motor on them, the washing machine was run by hand or a scrub-board was used. Throw away diapers must have been a real relief to the mothers.

When the men were gone to exchange work with the neighbors, gone for supplies, or working off-season at a sawmill for a little extra money or for lumber to build with, the wife was left with an extra load.

Most of the pioneers had a few cows that needed feeding, and usually one that could be milked so the family had fresh milk and even some butter. The chickens had to be taken care of to maintain a good supply of eggs for the family and most of the time there were a few pigs that needed feeding and water, which usually had to be carried in five gallon buckets.

After the day's chores were done, the water barrel full of snow, the wood box full and kids in bed, there were always clothes or socks to mend or a new dress to be made or maybe a letter that needed to be written. With mail only once a week, those letters couldn't be forgotten.

When the man of the house returned, it was expected that the house should be clean and everything in tip top shape. There was very little complaining or statements like, "I just wouldn't do that." Those women understood that for their mental survival they had to accept the idea that they would do all they could and the best they could, therefore they gained respect and appreciation.

There were few fights between husbands and wives as they were and had to be committed to each other. They needed each other in every way and what a joy to feel needed.

I don't think enough can be said about the pioneer women of all districts and countries.

Worsley was the place where most people went on mail day. It had a post office and a general store with a telephone switch board in it. If you needed to make a long distance telephone call, you went there and the storekeeper, Mr. Nicholson would plug in the phone to connect to another switch board in a family's home in Hines Creek. This was a twenty-four hour switchboard operated by the mother of the home who also was raising her five children. If the call needed to go beyond Hines Creek, she'd plug in to Peace River and on down the line. Sometimes it would take several minutes to be connected to your party.

The little store sold a lot of groceries to the people in the area - on credit, with no interest charges. Some were farmers, homesteaders, trappers and loggers and when they had some crop, lumber, furs or some other produce, they'd pay their bills. There was a garage that did repairs on any kind of vehicle or machinery that needed repairing and also delivered gas to farmers. A lot of their business operated the same way as the grocery store.

Worsley also had a nurse station to take care of the sick, deliver some babies and do some repairs on people. That was a real asset to the community as it was so isolated and far from a doctor or hospital. The school had teachers and classrooms from grades one to twelve. There was another grocery store and a hotel.

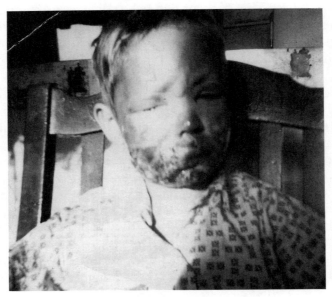

Manny, "My little man's burned face"

Jerry with deer he had to finish off with his jack knife

Chapter 10
Our First Years at Worsley

In the fall it was time for school to start and that meant Dudley K, Jody and I would be starting at a new school and many opportunities to make new friends.

I had finished grade ten in Texas. Now it was grade eleven with a totally different kind of credit system. I knew I would have lots of work to do to make the change.

For two months I needed all the spare time I had at home working on my school work. I knew my Dad needed me to help him. He was by himself, trying to get used to making a living from livestock, and moving on to a place where no provisions had been made to accommodate any. That meant that there were lots of things that had to be done before winter. I really couldn't concentrate on my school work knowing this, so I chose to drop out of school and do what I could to help him.

In a new country with very little money and no credit, there was very little chance of getting much livestock for winter. We managed to buy a few cows and soon winter was upon us. It got cold. Some friends helped us get some moose meat for the winter and I shot a deer, so we were in good shape for meat.

When a local sawmill started up for the winter, my Dad and I saw an opportunity to get a job there. It was a great experience for a boy of seventeen. It got bitter cold for a while that winter, the temperature went to sixty below zero and stayed there for about a month. Sawmill work was hard work and by the time supper was over, there were a lot of stories to be told in the bunkhouse.

With only a single board wall and no insulation in it, you might think people would freeze in it; but with snow banked up high around the outside walls and a big wood heater, it was all right until the fire went out, then you really appreciated a warm bed roll!

There were two bunk houses for the men to stay in. These had single bunks all around the walls with a big wood heater in the center of the room. The toilets were all outside and of course no heat in them. Some couples had their own small cabins to stay in. Then, there was the cook house, with a long table in it and a big wood cook stove. There was always lots of good food including fresh baked bread. What a welcome sight at the end of a long day out in the cold.

To most of the people in the community, electricity was still just a dream, thus block heaters were of no use. So most of them took the battery from their vehicle into their house each night or their vehicle wouldn't start on a cold morning to get to work. Another way to get a vehicle going on a very cold morning was to put hot coals from the wood heater under the motor to warm up the oil. So, by staying in camp, the entire crew was ready to go to work at the same time every day.

On February 14, 1958, our little log house caught fire and burned. Most of our personal belongings were burned. Mother interpreted the fire as a direct sign that God did not want us living here and away from family.

But before the next night, the neighbors had all gotten together and gave us food, money, clothes and pulled a bunkhouse into the yard so we could be quite comfortable.

When your friends and neighbors treat you with so much care, giving of themselves what they had to give, I knew this was "home" and a country and community worth putting down roots in. I was convinced that I would not have to walk alone, surrounded by people like that.

When spring came, we had enough money to pay our bills and enough left over to buy five hundred little turkeys that we were going to raise and sell in the fall. Little turkeys are very delicate and we lost a lot of them. When it was time to sell them, we made a deck in the old truck we had moved with and on the way to Edmonton, the motor went out of the truck.

Being stranded on the road with a load of live turkeys was a different experience, but with another tractor hooked on to our trailer, we delivered the turkeys in good shape and had enough money to pay a few bills.

The next year in August, a forest fire broke out so the forestry department picked up some local people to go to the fire. We were flown in by helicopter. By midnight we had gone about half way around the fire putting it out, then we decided to go to sleep for a while. We had a tent and each one had a gray wool blanket. We had seen some bears on the way in, so when we laid down the talk turned to bears.

After a while the guy by the door crawled out and around the tent, took his finger and made a ripping sound down the tent. Well, the one on my left was a very nervous person and he let out a yell and was airborne instantly. Allen landed on the other side of me never again to sleep close to the wall of a tent.

The next day the wind came up and the fire really spread. That fire was not put out until the snow came.

We had a fairly good crop that year and when fall came Daddy thought sheep would be a good thing for us to have, so he borrowed money on his life insurance and we bought some sheep.

Hauling the sheep home in the truck over the Peace River at Clayhurst on ice was rather exiting. There was no bridge there at that time. I could just see this whole thing going through the ice and into the river. But, I needn't have feared for the ice was very thick and all arrived safely at home.

I had gotten to be good friends with a young man whose name was Ken Rohl. His parents had a general store in Worsley and he was a great help for them. When their store burned to the ground, they had quite a loss as they had no insurance on it. When Ken moved away it left a real emptiness in my heart. I have noticed that the kind of friend that a young man chooses can set the stage for his whole life.

Chapter 11
My Accident

On Sunday morning February 2, 1959, two of my friends and I were returning from a trip to Texas when we hit a snow storm in Oklahoma and had a wreck.

I remember that snow was hitting me in the face, people were talking funny, I was stuffed in the back seat of a car and off we went. My left thigh was broken and it seemed like a long way to the hospital.

I lay on a bed for four days with a pail of sand tied to my foot. What a situation to try to get any sleep in. Then Blue showed up. I told him, "Go get a doctor and get him to fix my leg, I can't stand it like this!" He found the doctor playing golf, brought him back and he fixed my leg with a plate and five gold screws. He told me I'd always be worth a little bit.

Days later, we were back at Blue's place in Texas. I had quite a time changing the motor and transmission from one car to another. I had some other major changes to make too and found it rather hard with a cast from my ankle to my waist, to get from a vertical to a horizontal position that I had to do several times.

I thought about the long trip to Worsley, Alberta in a car with a cast like this and knew it would not be a fun trip. The doctor had informed me that I would have to wear it for five months.

I learned to appreciate Blue and Betty in a new way. They had taken good care of me and given me a home. I was so thankful that I had a caring family in my time of need.

I thought about the lady in Woodward, Oklahoma who had come to the hospital for six days in a row and just tried to encourage me and read from the Bible to me every day. I had forgotten to thank her for what she'd done and worst of all, I had forgotten her name, so she could never know what an encouragement she had been to me.

It was on the way to that hospital that I had recommited my life to the Lord. He had surely spared my life. With a bloody face and one leg laying sideways I must have been quite a sight.

I was ready to take that long, hard trip back to Worsley, Mother flew down to drive me back and we headed for home!

It was lambing time when we got there and every extra square foot in our little house had a little lamb getting warmed up or getting a bottle of milk. As soon as they got warm and strong, out they went and in came some more. Being on crutches, I wasn't much help outside with anything.

One of our friends told Daddy about a place on the banks of the Peace River that would be a good place for the sheep for the summer. It was decided that his and our sheep would go there together for the summer of 1959. He knew a man that would be willing and was very capable to go with the sheep and care for them. This man had horses and a cabin there. The man's name was Dick Dixon.

After the mud was gone and the grass was coming, all the sheep were taken to the hills. The summer venture was about to begin.

It was soon shearing time and that was done on the spot. A few sheep were kept back each day to be sheared. Every night they were all put in a big log holding pen to keep tally on them.

The bears and coyotes were having a hay day. Sheep were disappearing every day. Some of the ewes were showing up with their udder ripped off and the little lambs had to steal milk from another mother to survive. The bears were doing this for the milk. After an inspection was done on a dead bear, the proof was there, for in his stomach there were three udders from the ewes.

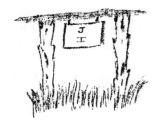

Chapter Twelve

Alberta Rose

Soon it was time for the little lambs tails to be docked, as this improved the growth rate. Daddy came home one night talking about the girl down at the sheep camp helping her Dad dock the lambs' tails. I decided right then, I just had to meet this girl.

Finally, the time had come to get this cast off so I could do something. I got the cast off and made plans to go help shear sheep.

It was tough going downhill on crutches and getting my toes stuck under roots in the trail. My knee didn't bend very much after being in a cast for so long but after a few flips, I made it to the bottom where the sheep camp was.

The sheep were strong from traveling in the hills and very hard to hold down. I couldn't catch them but Daddy would catch one and put it on a little table we made. Then I could shear them with a pair of hand shears. It was good to see the last one done.

The wool was put in big bags, loaded onto pack horses, hauled up the hills, loaded into a wagon pulled by a tractor for six miles, then finally into a truck to be taken out to Edmonton where it was sold by the pound.

One Sunday we planned to have a picnic and worship service on the banks of the Peace River. My Mother and some of our neighbors from Worsley drove as far as they could to our camp to meet us, the sheep shearing crew.

What a gorgeous day it turned out to be. The picnic lunch was wonderful as was the service. This girl I'd been dying to meet was also there making an impression on me that would last the rest of my life.

Through the summer, I learned to appreciate the man that was looking after our sheep. I was impressed by his horsemanship, many capabilities, his gentle way, and his adaptability to cope with whatever came along. Also that daughter of his they called "Rosie" was becoming of special interest to me. We began to see a bit of each other and it seemed that we had a lot of things in common.

With making feed for the winter, a periodic trip to the sheep camp and getting to know this new found Alberta Rose, summer was swiftly passing by.

Word came that my Mother's Father had Leukemia and he was not feeling very well. He had always been a very strong and healthy man. He was also a very kind and patient man. Years ago he had gotten into trouble with his Dad for killing a coon in his yard. His Dad had said that any time he couldn't find a coon to hunt at night with his hounds, he could always find this specific one and now his son had killed it. His Dad was only in his eighties and needed this night time sport for some excitement in his life.

By fall the bears and coyotes had taken a real toll on our sheep numbers; it looked pretty grim. We had a few yearling steers that summer too. They were also missing and no one had seen them for quite some time. We suppoed they had drifted west and we knew that soon we would have to go looking for them.

Mother and Daddy had gone to visit her ailing Father in Texas and it was my responsibility to get the sheep home while they were gone. Fall was here and winter was coming right behind it.

With the sheep all home, I knew we had to go back and try to find the lost steers. We made our plans. Rose's Mom and Dad and I were going to find them. We needed horses to ride and one to pack our food and gear.

Rose's Mom, Florence, was a half Cree Indian and she knew what we needed for a week of travel. Part of this meant cooking our bread that is called "bannock" by the campfire.

Rose's Dad, known as Dick to everyone was a great outdoorsman. He had come to the Peace River country for the pioneer lifestyle. He had trapped and homesteaded, clearing the land by hand, had some cattle and raised nine children. The oldest son was killed in a sawmill accident at the age of seventeen.

Life had some tough spots in it for Florence with no electricity or running water and a big family to feed and keep clean. Florence was a very ambitious, hard working woman that grew a big garden every year and enjoyed very much the sort of expedition we were about to go on.

Our grazing permit was on the north side of the Peace River, in unsurveyed, rough terrain. The second day of our trip, we were heading west in the Many Islands area, with Dick in the lead. All of a sudden a black bear came charging down the hill straight for us! Our horses spooked and almost unloaded us. Then the bear seemed to realize there were four big animals and instantly turned tail at a dead run. We weren't really sure what he had on his mind but we were sure glad he changed it.

We camped by a little creek that night. The next morning we had our breakfast and were ready to go shortly after day light. We had to climb a steep bank to get back out from the creek. Florence was almost to the top when the cinch on her saddle broke. She came tumbling backward off her horse, still in the saddle, rolling and tumbling all the way back to the bottom of the creek. She did not get hurt but we sure had a very unhappy cook for a while. Dick had some spare rope in his pack with which he repaired the cinch and we were soon going again. This time, she wouldn't ride up the steep hill, she walked.

It wasn't until the fourth day that we found the cattle. They were all together but sure were spooky. It took quite a while to get them to travel in the same direction. But, two days later we had them safely home. This had been another great learning experience for me and I was very happy that I didn't have to do it alone.

Dick and Florence went home to get ready for winter. Getting up a big wood pile was quite a project for Dick. This was before chain saws came into the picture and he had to cut the trees by hand or with a Swede saw. Then he'd load them onto a sleigh that his team of horses could pull home. When he had several loads in a pile, it was then time to saw wood. He had an old 1530 McCormick Deering tractor with a pulley on it. He would put a big wide belt from the pulley and over to the bush saw with a big blade on that. He didn't have antifreeze for the tractor so he warmed up the water for the motor. When the sawing was done, he would drain the water back out so as not to freeze up and break the motor.

It took four people to have a good wood cutting crew. Each log had to picked up and carried to the saw where it was cut in block size for the wood stove. One person had to catch the blocks as they were cut and throw them into a pile. By the end of that day, there would be a big enough wood pile to last for the winter. Of course, getting up a big wood pile was just one of the many tasks of preparing for what could be a long winter.

My Grandpa Pope was getting progressively worse. My Mother wanted to be near him in his last days. The sheep venture had not been a good one, so my folks decided to move back to Texas. Our farm there had not sold yet so they had a place to go to.

I didn't want to move back there now. This country was my home and I was already a part of it. I didn't see much future there for a young man that had not finished high school, so I made up my mind I was staying.

I knew within a month after I'd met my Rose that I had met my match and we would spend the rest of our lives together. We talked about it. We were both very young, I was nineteen and she was seventeen.

We decided with a lot of hard work together we could have a good life. We planned our wedding for October 24, 1959.

Dad traded the sheep for pigs and made plans to leave. He had grown to love the country and people and felt in his heart that the Lord wanted him here. To pack up and leave must have been very hard for him. Plans were made that I would take care of the pigs and rent his half section of land in Worsley on half shares. He had some equipment he would leave here.

We had a small, beautiful wedding in the home of Rose's older sister, Joyce in Fairview, Alberta. It was a cold, rainy day but a wonderful event as we exchanged the vows and commitment to each other that down through the years would hold us together. The girl I had met down at the sheep camp was now to be the light of my life and life long companion.

A week later Mother, Daddy, Jody, K ("Soup"), Charlotte and Dick left for Texas. I had often thought about people who had to say goodbye to their loved ones as they went off to war to fight for their country; not knowing what lay in store or if they would ever see each other again. I understood the feelings of their heart, a kind of lonely, empty feeling.

About the only things Rose and I had, was a deep love and commitment for each other and a lot of friends with no money either. One friend had given me a job driving his tractor at night working his land behind the combine to earn enough money to buy Rose a wedding ring. Life was good for us. We had all the necessities except a wood pile, so we got busy and stored up our winter's wood.

An old friend had once said, "You show me the woman that sleeps on the man's arm, and I'll tell you if I'll do any business with him." It wasn't long and I knew the Lord had helped me find a good woman. We enjoyed doing things and being together.

We knew we needed a little money, so I got a job driving a neighbor's truck hauling grain for some of the farmers in the area.

On December 3, 1959, I was hauling some of my Dad's grain to town when I had another bad accident. I lost the middle two fingers off my right hand in the grain auger that loaded grain into the truck.

This auger was the kind that was fastened onto the truck. It had a shaft that had a mean flop to it. I thought I could straighten it out a bit. I shouldn't have tried this because my gloves were damp and they stuck to the cold iron. I got my left hand free, grabbed onto the granary door with it, leaned back and pulled with all my strength. I know I could have lost my whole arm but this ordeal cost me the two middle fingers from my right hand. What a pitiful sight as I watched one complete finger with long tendons flopping around on that auger shaft. What a start off for newly weds!

At the very time of the accident, a couple drove into the yard selling Watkins Products. When they saw what happened, they drove Rose and me to the neighbors.

This special neighbor, Bowden then drove us to the nurse in Worsley two miles away. After the nurse had cleaned and bandaged my hand and gave me a pain killer, Bowden drove us to the hospital sixty miles away. I can't say as I remember much of that trip. I do remember it was painful.

Before Rose got home that night, another very thoughtful neighbor, Edmond came over and took the fingers from the auger and put them in a little jar of alcohol. He gave them to me after I got home.

These have come in handy many times, as we found that sometimes if an unexpected bunch of guests arrived in time for supper, and we might run a little short of food, if we passed the little jar around for everyone to have a look, we always had plenty of food for everyone.

Well, after a week in the hospital, I was not only without any money, I now had a three hundred dollar doctor bill to pay for services rendered. It took a year to get him paid. He was very patient with me and was always happy when I could pay a little on my bill.

A friend suggested that I go see if Welfare would help out a bit with my handicapped condition. In my interview with them, I told them about the doctor bill I owed and a payment I needed to make on my pickup. They said they were very sorry but were unable to help. "So now," I thought, "we are really going to see what it's like to get by with no money coming in and no chance of any for a good while".

We got an invitation to go to Texas and spend the winter with my folks and do what we could to help there. We sold Daddy's pigs and caught a ride to Edmonton with a friend. Then we took the rest of our money and bought two bus tickets to Texas. We arrived just before Christmas, after traveling four days and nights by bus.

After about a week in Texas, my hand started to smell kind of bad. When we unwrapped it, we found the skin graft hadn't worked. The piece they had taken from my stomach for the graft had turned all black. I went to see a doctor to get a new verdict on it and he suggested a new skin graft. I thought about that and how the other doctor had taken a piece from my stomach three inches wide by five inches long; he must have thought he was dealing with rough lumber. I decided I couldn't spare that much again so I chose to let it heal over on it's own. Within a month a very thin layer of skin had formed so I knew it would be O.K.

We helped with the field work and looked after the cattle. I was glad to be able to help Blue and Betty a little, as I felt I was indebted to them for looking after me when I had my leg broken. Blue also had married a wonderful woman. It is great when you can appreciate your relatives. Daddy was busy building houses to sell to make a little money and Mother was happy to be back close to her family. They both have come from large families and have many relatives.

Rose got to meet all four of my Grandparents as well as lots of relatives. She was able to see a lot of things that without the accident she would not have seen. I have never seen anything that was all bad yet. Everything has some good in it. Sometimes we just have to look hard to see the good.

Winter went fast. I was getting used to getting along without two fingers and being very thankful for what I had left. Rose was getting used to be being married to a handicapped man.

In March, Mother and Daddy bought us tickets to return to Edmonton by train and from there to Hines Creek by bus. We counted our money in Edmonton and we decided we could spare enough for Rose to have half a grapefruit because she kept saying she was famished. When we reached Hines Creek, we had enough to buy us each a hamburger. We caught a ride with some friends to our home in Worsley. It sure felt good to be back home!

We had to sell some potatoes that Dick and Florence had kept for us through the winter to get some money to repair the differential in our pickup. Our neighbors were good to us. One good neighbor sold us seed on credit. The store owner gave us groceries on credit and the garage owners gave us gas on credit. All these wonderful people gave credit not knowing if they'd ever get paid; but that is the way it is in a pioneer country. There is a trust and with that trust, a non written commitment to pay.

We had a good crop that year and in mid summer, I was able to get a job helping build a house for the Forestry Department to get a few dollars. That was really appreciated. I have a great appreciation for the people who took a chance on us.

Rose told me, years later, that one day she had a craving for some strawberry jam. Because we were buying groceries on credit we tried to keep our spending as low as possible. So after eating her fill, she realized if she showed me the can, I would wonder what happened to the rest of it, so she kept it hid from me until she'd cleaned the whole can up by herself. Later on, her conscience got to bothering her and she told me about it. We both had a good laugh about it.

One thing I knew I was going to miss, was our worship service time on Sunday like we always had at home. But Rose and I found a place to worship on Sunday at the home of a friend, or at her parent's place. This was a good time in my life as I had to decide which direction I would lead my family. There are always people with differet aspects of your faith so I chose to look at the Bible myself and try to conclude what this life was all about.

We once had a milk cow, that sometimes when I went to get her, she'd stand behind a tree. As long as she had her head hid, she thought she was hidden. She taught me a good lesson; which is, we have to be smaller than something to hide behind it.

I knew there was no one to hide behind with my excuses. That motivated me to study for myself so I could put things in the right perspective and work on priorities. I knew that I was far from perfect and that the Lord had been so good to me and I dare not forget this.

Our first crop and garden were good. We had our harvest over and were ready for winter. We sold enough grain to pay all of our summer bills and bought a few cows.

On December 20, 1960, our first child, a son was born. We named him Manny Duane. What a great day that was for Rose and me. We had Christmas dinner in the hospital that year.

Soon my little family was home with me. What a long list of dreams I had. I had so much to teach my son and there were so many things we would do together.

Our little home wasn't very fancy or very big, but we had the opportunity to share it with several people who needed a place to stay, some for a few weeks, some a few months. We had no TV so we sang a lot together. Over the years to follow we were privileged to sing for the community at a lot of funerals, anniversaries, weddings and Church specials.

In the summer of 1961, my family came from Texas to visit and help with harvest. Mother and the children returned to Texas when it came time for school, but Daddy stayed on to help. Both their Dads had passed away by now and Canada was still very much on Daddy's heart. Mother always did the best she could to make their life and marriage as good and pleasant as could be.

Rose drove the tractor with Manny zipped up inside her coat most of the time and Daddy rode on the binder making bundles. A bundle is an armful of feed with a string wrapped around it. After the bundles were made, we went along and took six or eight of these bundles and stood them up so the wind could blow through them and they could dry. This is called "stooking." When they were dried, we hauled them into the feed yard and made a big stack to be fed out in the winter.

Jerry and Rose Hale Wedding
October 24, 1959

Jerry and Rose Hale
25th Anniversary,
October 24, 1984

Chapter Thirteen
A New Opportunity

In August that year Mr. Bill Sherly who had known my Dad for a long time in Texas, came up and bought some land on the Peace River. An agreement was made that Rose and I would move to this new place, look after it and seventy cows that he would buy in the spring on shares. We did this for nine years.

I had filed on a Homestead that spring, which was located close enough so that I could work on it as time and money permitted. Daddy, Mother, K, Charlotte and Dick would be moving back to Canada in the spring to stay and that was good news for me.

After we had feed put up for the winter, the land needed cultivating at this new place that we would be moving to in the spring. We put a box on the cultivator, some necessities we would need for a week, Rose and Manny got in the box and away we went. We left early in the morning and got to this new place just before dark. The old tractor I was driving didn't go very fast.

What a beautiful location on the banks of the Peace River. There were always lots of Saskatoon berries and Choke cherries growing wild and they made a delicious treat when a jar was brought out of the cellar for dessert with a meal.

This land was located at the end of the road and had a large tract of unsurveyed land to the west of it. This became our grazing lease for cattle in the summer for many years.

A week later we had the field work finished and were ready to return to Worsley. It had been an enjoyable week.

The previous owner, Herb was still living there. He was an old

Swedish fellow and had lived in a big log house by himself for many years. I really came to admire people like him with a real pioneer spirit. These people went to the end of the road and beyond, cleared out a piece of land and put it into production. They put into society, providing food and meat, with never a consideration of taking more out than they were putting in. They went through some real hardships to get supplies in and grain out to the train to be sold. Most of the transporting was done with a team and wagon or sleighs.

I thought to myself, "What a good way to be. To want to put in more than we take out. I'm sure that's the way our forefathers were and that's the way I want to be".

Manny spent his first birthday on the road to Texas. It was nice to have Christmas with a lot of relatives. Minus forty was kind of cold to start out on a trip like that with a little guy, but it turned out good.

We had some new neighbors who looked after our place. They were great people and became lifelong friends. I have noticed as we travel along on life's highway, we appreciate some people more as time goes on. Such was so with the Hellquists.

Well, spring had come again and is always such a welcome after a long winter and deep snow! When the snow begins to melt, little drops turn into trickles, trickles into streams, streams into rivers, and into the ocean. Bare ground starts showing, green grass starts growing and flowers and birds come. It's good to be alive.

It was time to gather the cattle together and start the drive to their new home. They had been purchased as planned and delivered by truck to Worsley. The grass was starting to grow on the hills and it was time to move them. A neighbor was hired with a team and wagon to haul the calves, as some were too small to travel. It would be a day and a half trip if all went well.

Rose made us a big stew because she knew there wouldn't be much cooking time on the trail and she couldn't go along this time. The stew was loaded in the front of the wagon with the bedding and other food. It took a while to get everything organized and for the mothers to realize that their babies were in the wagon; then we were off.

There was a great bunch of guys helping move these cattle. This would become an annual event for many years to come, because Daddy's cattle always spent the summer with the "share" cattle I had. His had to be moved every spring to the grass. This was one of the highlights of the year.

Sometime in the afternoon the lid bounced off the big pot of stew. The partition that divided the baby calves from the front section wasn't quite high enough and one of the calves added to the stew.

The alert teamster saw what happened and took a big spoon and scooped out what he could, then mixed the rest. After supper was over, Cliff told us about it and went on to say, "I knew that was our food for supper and I really had no choice." He ate as much as anyone and there was none to throw away. Rose was glad that she had missed that stew!

The cattle were glad to get to the green grass. It had been a tough trip on them through lots of water and mud. What a great reunion when the cows and calves were all paired up again. It sure felt good to a bunch of tired cowboys too, to lie on a dry bed before we struck out again.

That summer was to be packed full of different activities. Rose and I had to make our move now that the cattle were already there. This new place was about twenty miles from an all-weather road and when it rained, it made for a tough trip. At this new residence, the log house was great until it started to rain and then there was not a thing in the house that didn't get wet. The ceiling had round poles with moss and dirt on top. It would drip inside for two days after it quit raining.

With a three hundred gallon tank on a wagon and a hose through the wall, we had running water at least at one tap. We had a wood stove to cook on and Rose put out many a good meal. We also had a good garden spot and she soon had a garden on the way.

Very few fences meant a lot of hours on a horse to keep track of the cattle.

On June 8, 1962, Manny's little sister, Darla Annette was born. What a great blessing to us and what a dream list Rose had for her and her little daughter.

I will never forget the day that I got the news about my new daughter. Because of the very poor condition our road got into when it rained, I had taken Rose and left her in Fairview to await the birth of our baby. Mrs. Costley was very happy to have her stay with her. Manny stayed at Grandma and Grandpa Dixon s. That morning Grandpa Dixon came driving his old truck and Grandma sitting up in there holding Manny. He was wearing a little cap with a big note pinned on the front of it that read, "Hi Dad, I have a new sister. She weighed nine seven." What a happy moment in a man's life to know all went well, and again, I thanked the Lord.

When you are young and healthy, you can do a lot of work in a day, especially when the days are so long. New corrals and fences had to be built. Posts had to be cut and sharpened on one end so we could drive them into the ground. K, myself and one of Rose's brothers, Ken drove lot of posts by hand, taking turns at swinging the post mall. The ground was very hard and dry. If we had been swinging at rocks, we would have had a pile of rocks busted.

Mr. Sherly's son, Billy Bob and his friend came up in June to build a hay shed. Then when we made square bales of hay we could store it under a roof and it kept better.

Mr.Sherly hired another crew to build a new house for us. As there were no restaurants close by, Rose burned a pile of wood in the old stove cooking to keep everyone fed.

We had some good neighbors here too. One day one of the neighbor women, Ruth came driving in with a tractor to bring Rose a beautiful bouquet of flowers. The Wutzkes became very special neighbors to us.

One of our neighbors wanted to go to the stampede that summer and take his family for a week. He had his problems arranging this. He had a milk cow that needed looking after, so he turned the cow and calf out to roam together. Then there was the pig that needed care, so he shot the dog and threw it over into the pig pen so the pig had something to eat. He then took a five gallon pail, and poked a little hole in the bottom so it would drip, filled it with water, hung it in the corner of the pig pen in a tree and away they went to the stampede.

He had no license on his truck and when the cop stopped him, he said he was trying out this truck to see if he wanted to buy it. The cop supposed it a likely story and let him carry on.

He was a man of much capability. He had traded a team of horses for his wife and a week later, he borrowed the horses and sold them because he needed grocery money. This man was always full of stories and good for a laugh.

One spring, the high water had washed a big culvert out of the road, so we put logs across the wash-out so we could drive across with a tractor to get supplies in. Well, Jim needed to get across but didn't make it. His tractor fell in the creek. The water was high. He had two headlights mounted on top of his radiator and the lights were the only thing sticking out. He swam to shore and climbed back on the road.

His father-in-law had thought it best not to cross and had watched the whole episode. He asked, "Jim, are you stuck?" When Jim told me what happened he thought it was a big joke and we had a big laugh. I've often thought if he could have sold his laugh, he'd have been a millionaire. It seemed like it came up from his toes.

One year Carl Wutzke knew that Jim didn't have many spare dollars so he offered to give him a little wheat for Christmas money for the kids. That sounded like a great offer so Jim filled his pickup box full of wheat and blew out both back tires before he got to town. So much for Christmas money for the kids!

The last fight that he and his wife had, ended their togetherness. He threw the wife and kids out. Then everything else he could throw out went into a pile in the yard and he burned it. Two days later his wife walked out across the field to where Rose was raking hay and asked if she had any milk to spare for her baby. She and her children had moved into an empty little log cabin and had been there with no food for two days. Those people had it very rough.

It would take a big book to write about all of our good neighbors and the good things they did for us. Some things are never to be forgotten. Like the man that came to visit one day and he had a match stick in each eye to hold his lids open. I thought it must be hard to see around them.

"It's haying time, gang, so let's get rolling, the sun's been up for an hour!" We had just had a big breakfast of sourdough hotcakes right off the wood stove.

We had a bunch of hay down. Some was raked and we were going to start baling hay today. It was short but we needed all there was out there. We had to take turns stacking it on the wagon and then stacking it in the shed. We were a young crew and full of ambition.

Rose had her hands full that day after cooking a big breakfast for the haying crew, which was seven that day. There were also two guys building the shed, three building the new house and probably one or two extras before the day was through, two small children and no electrical appliances to work with.

The hay was dry and the baling went well. One person was mowing, one raking, one driving the tractor baling and one stacking bales on the wagon behind the baler just as fast as they were made. One wagon was always on the way to the hay shed to be unloaded and stacked in the shed by two people and one wagon on the way back. It took three wagons to make it work right.

Without some people being full of fun, jobs get boring after a while. Right after lunch, we headed back to the hay field. Rose's brother, Keith always had lots of fun. His sister, Shirley was driving the tractor pulling the wagon and they were in high gear. Wesley was standing up on the flat deck; it was smoother that way. Keith had a plan. He stood on the back of the tractor and when the time

56

and place was just right, with his toe he pulled the pin out of the hitch unhooking the wagon from the tractor.

Everything worked as planned. The wagon tongue stuck in the ground and stopped immediately. Poor Wes went flying through the air and scooped up a bunch of dirt with his face. It's a miracle he didn't get killed!

He couldn't understand why that trailer came unhooked, it had never done that before. Keith told him it was safer riding on the tractor with him next time.

By the end of the week we had put four thousand bales in the new shed. Later we put up an equal amount of straw for the winter feed.

Next it was time to get a few acres broke on the "Homestead" so we could seed it the next spring. Part of the first ten acre field was open and the rest we cleared by hand. The roots and stumps we picked and put in piles, then we burned them. The land was broken with a one bottom plow and disked several times. Finally, it was ready for spring seeding.

That was a big accomplishment. Ten acres on our own land that had already cost fifty dollars. I had to clear and put into production, one hundred and twenty acres of the three hundred and twenty acres before the Government would give me a clear title to this half section.

With fencing done for the summer we made plans to cut posts once the ground froze so we could go through the wet country to spread them out. We knew some of the country that had to be fenced to enclose and contain the cattle was impossible to haul posts and wire over, unless it was frozen.

We had enough hay for the winter. We'd had a very good garden and it was harvested. Rose had canned lots of saskatoons and vegetables.

Our new house was finished and it was time to move into it. We had installed a wood and coal heater in the basement and had a big round hole with a grate on it for the heat to come up through. It was going to be warm and nothing inside would get wet when it rained. I bought Rose a second hand propane refrigerator and cook stove. We had a hand pump on the cupboard that pumped water from a cistern in the basement. It was like a little bit of heaven!

After a big wood pile was cut and put in a shed, I went hunting and shot a moose for winter meat. As moose were plentiful and money short, we lived on moose meat for several years.

We sold the calves and after the split, my share was a big check for eight hundred and twenty dollars. It was a good thing Rose had put in a big garden that year.

We had borrowed one thousand dollars and bought four yearlings in the spring. One of them fell over a cliff and broke his back. Ken and I took some baler twine down to the river and built a raft.

Then we loaded this calf on it with plans to float it down the river four miles to where there was a trail coming down to the river. This was our only means of getting him out.

So we shoved off, our little Border Collie had a rather anxious look on her face. With long poles and the help of the current, two hours later we were where we could get to with a tractor and trailer. We decided we couldn't save the calf so we had meat for the summer.

After the sale of the other three, there was just enough money left to pay the debt at the bank. Credit was good; pockets were empty.

Older people can teach us a lot if we are willing to learn. I was discussing finances with an old friend one day and he said, "If you can pay your bills every year, you are doing great." It took many years until I could understand that.

I also asked him what it took to be successful in the cattle business. His answer over the years would apply to many things. He said, "If you want to be a successful cattle man, you get your advice from a successful cattle man."

A lot of people can tell you what not to do, but a sheep man can't tell you how to be successful in cattle and a dentist can't tell you how to be successful at farming. It's kind of hard for a person to give you advice on how to raise children if they haven't successfully done it or to give marriage counseling if they aren't having a successful marriage. I have appreciated older people giving me advice even sometimes when it was unsolicited.

It was starting to get cold now but we needed some supplies and the road was still good, so we decided to go to town. We stopped at our old friend Herb Lund's to see if he needed anything from town.

His cabin was cold and he was in bed with a bad cough. He didn't need anything and didn't want to go see a doctor. He said, "I'll come all right." But he wondered if I could cook him some eggs, so I did. I noticed some blood in his garbage can and thought he must have pneumonia.

I checked with the nurse in town and she said there was no use in her going out to see him, he needed to be in the hospital. On our way home we stopped again. I could see he was worse, but no, he still didn't want to go to the hospital.

He had been a strong man and a hard worker. He told me of the time there was only one woman in the area and all the bachelors kind of liked her. One man was very jealous and thought Herb was getting ahead of him, so he waited outside his barn door one night with a neck yoke, that's the wooden part that goes between a team of horses and holds up the front of the long pole that goes between them.

Anyway when Herb came out, his neighbor let him have it over the head and ran. He thought he had eliminated his opposition. Herb said when he came to, he had a big knot on his head and he couldn't wear a cap for quite some time.

Herb was the one who had previously owned this new place we were living on. He told me one time there was a grave down in the corner of a certain field and said, "You can't plow there after dark, I tried it once and when I got to a certain place, something knocked me right off so don't go there at night." He had been riding on a plow with four horses pulling it.

Well, we talked him into going to our place. After we got him, the kids and the groceries all inside he wanted a warm glass of milk. I went to milk the cow while Rose fed and put the kids to bed. The thermometer was sitting on minus thirty. It was sure good to be home, a warm fire and the chores done for the day.

When I came back in, I looked at Herb and told him, "Herb, I'm taking you to the hospital." I could see a change in him just while I was out doing the chores. He was very weak and just mumbled something.

Rose got on one side and me on the other and we started for the door. His head slumped forward and he passed out. He was heavy and we had a hard time getting him down the stairs and into the pickup. It was a cold trip that night not knowing if my passenger was dead or not. I checked his pulse periodically. There was nothing to do but get him there as quick as possible. We had no phone to call for help.

They put him on oxygen immediately an said, "It doesn't look good." He was unconscious so I knew there was nothing else I could do and my family might need me at home.

Early next morning a lady that drove a taxi came and told us that he had not made it through the night. One more old pioneer was gone. The lady that brought the word owned a hardware store with her husband in Hines Creek and they did many such deeds for many people for many years. I suppose they were not appreciated by some, but they were appreciated by most people and respected for the many years of service to the pioneer people. Griep's Hardware has been a landmark in Hines Creek and was owned by Margaret and Alfie Griep.

Calving time was always a great time. You know spring is close. You can watch these little calves take their first breath and then get up on wobbly legs with an instinct to get some milk for nourishment to sustain them in cold weather.

The first milk is so important to the new born to help build an immune system. Some cows had lots of milk and we learned to get some milk from some of these to have on hand for some of the little ones whose mother either had very little milk or didn't want this strange looking new creature. Convincing a cow that she should love her own baby was sometimes a "trying on the patience time."

Some cold nights some little guys would get the tips of their ears or the end of their tail froze which would fall off later. We practically lived with the cattle at calving time. The older cows usually knew enough to lick their baby dry and when it was cold weather this was pretty important. A dry calf with a full stomach can take a lot of cold weather.

Mr. Sherly, Sr. came up in the spring to see how we were doing in this new venture. He was the father of the one we were in shares with. The snow was pretty deep yet. He looked at the feed pile, and you could already see over the top of it and then at me and said, "Jerry, the Lord is going to have both arms around your neck if you're going to make it to grass with these cows!"

Spring came early that year. There was lots of old grass left from the year before. This is very important because if the cattle can get some of the old grass the new growth won't just pass on through them like water, as it is mostly water anyway.

The fencing was well under way. We used a team of horses to pull a little cart to unroll the wire and pounded in the posts by hand. We had about six miles to fence on our schedule that summer.

We had a tent set up for "home" while we were fencing. When we got to camp one particular night, our tent had been ripped down and the oats we had in bags for the horses were gone. A little trail of oats led off into the bush and at the end of the trail, an empty sack. Most of our food was gone. All the tin cans had holes in them.

Rose rode in on a horse about that time and saw all this mess. She was bringing me some rubber boots as we had lots of mud and water to work in. We were camped about five miles from our home. Her Dad was the teamster on this project. While we were cleaning up, my little gray horse let out a big snort. I knew he had smelled a bear.

I grabbed my gun and waited. He soon showed up, which would have been better for him if he hadn't. We knew he was the one who had caused all the damage, because he was full of oats and raisins.

We made a deal with Dick to spend the summer with the cattle and he continued to do this for several summers. One day he came riding in and said, "Today, I am a very sick man. I did something today I didn't think I'd ever do. I was checking how far west the cattle were and as I came over the ridge, there was a big black bear." We had been having lots of trouble with bears getting the young calves. He went on to say, "After I shot it and went down to it, it was one of the black cows." So he had dressed it out and knew he needed help to get it out. We needed meat anyway so it wasn't wasted.

We built a log cabin for him to stay in out in the middle of the lease. It was also a good dry place to store salt for the cattle and it took lots of it.

It was getting cold again and close to winter, time to go get some winter's meat. One particular day was going to have a new experience for me, something that I had never heard of, except on TV. We were hunting with horses, a friend and myself. He shot a nice buck deer and just then, I looked towards the river. I saw a moose that the shot had spooked, running up a ridge.

I told my friend that I was going to see if I could intercept it, so up on my horse and at a run we went. I thought I was getting close to where he would come up so I pulled my gun from the scabbard and pumped in a shell. I had never shot off this horse before and I didn't know just what would happen. I had tried it before on another horse, that one had unloaded me and I had to walk home.

I was just ready when the moose jumped out into the trail in front of me. The horse thought we were going to rope it and gave it all he had. I pulled the gun up to shoot, but my horse was going up and down at a dead run and the moose fifty feet in front was going up and down, but not in time with me and my horse.

I thought, "I have seen people do this before in western movies with pistols, I should be able to do this easy with a rifle." I pulled the trigger.

The moose never slowed up, old Partner just shook his head but he never missed a beat, just full steam ahead. He saw the gun come up again and just turned his head way off to the left. He knew it was going to be a loud bang again but never slowed up. After the third shot the moose thought, enough of this and turned off into the bush without the loss of one hair. Then I really had questions of all the shows I'd seen in the movies.

The next day, I was up early and gone hunting again. I took a different horse this time. I had named her Cactus because every time she got in a little patch of cactus, she would go nuts. She was a big strong, blue roan that never seemed to tire.

We lived just beside a large parcel of unsurveyed government land, which was our grazing lease. This land laid along the north side of the Peace River and most of it was tree covered. We had made a few trails with a bull dozer which made nice access trails for the lease.

I was about six miles from home when I spotted a moose down over a very steep bank. I knew I didn't dare shoot off her, or I'd be left sitting on the ground, so I tied Cactus up to a tree. I sneaked to the edge of the hill and sure enough, the moose was still there. I took careful aim with my 300 savage lever action open sight rifle and down it went. I watched for a moment, feeling good that this old rifle would once again feed my family. Then, the moose got back on it's feet and I knew it wouldn't run away. After looking the situation over, I decided to make a circle around the moose. I thought perhaps if I spooked it, it might just climb that hill instead of me having to carry it up. It was a steep hill. My plan didn't work. The moose decided instead of climbing the steep hill, the first thing it should do was run over that guy carrying a rifle. I knew I had three small children and a wife counting on me so I put a bullet right between his eyes and dropped him there. Then, I stopped and thanked God once more for helping me. I knew it would be a big job butchering and packing all that meat up the hill. I asked him for some extra strength because it was already late afternoon.

Cactus could have helped me but when the ground is frozen and without horse shoes there was no way she could climb that steep hill. I knew she would be well rested by the time I was ready to go.

I tied the two hind quarters on to the horse's tail with a piece of rope. I had found out a few years before that a horse can pull lots from their tail. We didn't take long getting home once I got everything ready. Fresh tenderloins were a wonderful treat that night. My Rose really is a wonderful cook.

One fall, I was looking for meat. I only had one shell. I found a nice buck deer and shot from above him. Down he went. When I got to where he was, he jumped up and ran. He stopped again and laid down. I saw a big dry stick laying on the ground. I picked it up and sneaked up behind him. I was hoping I could knock him out by hitting him a hard blow between the horns. He jumped up again and ran. Then he laid down again. I was by myself so, "Now what am I going to do?" I never left a wounded animal so I had to do something. I wondered if I could hold him if I was able to get him by the horns. I've twisted a pretty big steer down so I have to try, I thought.

I sneaked up on him again, grabbed him by his horns and the wrestle was on. Deer have very sharp feet and he was trying very hard to get me, trying to shake me off his horns. We knocked over several little trees. I knew now I could not turn loose or he would kill me. He didn't know that I had a wife and kids at home that needed meat and I was there to stay. I could tell he was weakening fast and down he went. I had lost my skinning knife in this wrestle.

When I found I could hold him with one hand, I dug out my pocket knife and cut his throat. He was the largest buck I had ever killed. I had his head mounted and when it was ready to be picked up, I didn't have the thirty five dollars to redeem it, so a store owner bought it and hung it in his store which later burned with all it's contents.

Albert Arnold had been a good friend. He had no knee cap on one leg so he walked with one leg stiff. He had to swing it out to the side and in deep snow it was tough for him. He was the best moose hunter I ever saw. He could track a moose through grass and leaves and across other moose tracks, then walk up to it and shoot it.

He said one time he and his wife, with a child on her back, were in the bush when a forest fire started. After trying all day to stay ahead of it, with big packs on both their backs, and sparks flying all around them, they both tired out and couldn't go any farther. He said, "We stopped and prayed for God's help, then we went to sleep. In the morning we had two inches of new snow." He said he had slept on the cold ground so much that he had wrecked his knee and they had to take the knee cap out.

One year he had cut a big wood pile for a friend by hand and hauled and built a big bale stack for another. For years he had lived in the bush and after being attacked by a grizzly bear that bit a big hole in his leg and many other narrow escapes, on a trip to the city with a son in law, he was run into with a car and that accident had ended his life. He was a great old friend. He once told me about how two of his daughters were in Hines Creek one day and a man went nuts and shot and killed both of them.

The coal car had come in. Several of us had ordered a box car load together. We had a busy day getting ours home, helping others get theirs, plus a load for my parents who were gone to Texas at that time on business. Rose and I were staying at Worsley taking care of their livestock and Rose's sister, Shirley was looking after ours. It was thirty below zero that day in November. I had the last load of coal unloaded, the cattle fed, the cow milked, and Rose said, "Jerry, it's time to go." I knew what that meant and we made the sixty five mile drive into Fairview on time.

Our Alisa Rose made history that day as she was born the same day that President Kennedy was shot, November 22, 1963. Once again Rose had a long list of dreams with her new little daughter!

That winter I worked driving a Cat clearing brush. Rose had a big old horse called Riley. She would harness him up and hook him up to a sleigh. Then she'd drive him out to the hay stack and put on a load of bales to take out to the feed area. Riley knew what to do and would walk along while she cut the strings on the bales and kicked them off the sleigh. Sometimes Rose would feed right up to the house so the cows could pack the snow down. The cattle cleaned every straw up. We had no snow plow and this kept our yard packed.

By spring time, Riley could pull as many bales as you could load on the sleigh; but when the snow started to melt and bare patches of dirt showed up he really had to scratch to pull it. Most of the time you didn't need to touch the lines, just talk to him, he knew what to do.

The water hole had to be opened and this was a big job when the ice got thick and the dug out was getting low. Sometimes it took a lot of chopping to get to water and the cattle would be standing almost on top of you waiting for their drink.

The cow needed milking twice a day and chickens needed some care. The wood had to be carried in for the furnace. When I was working out, Rose had her hands full. We had no phone and for years only one vehicle.

When I had gotten caught up clearing land for other people, Mr. Basnett told me to take his Cat to our homestead and clear up some of our own land. We now had twenty acres in production. The second year we had crop on it. It froze on August 11 and finished off the crop, so no combining expenses were necessary that year. I told Mr. Basnett I had no money and couldn't do that. He said, "Well, go do it anyway, but when you get your first crop off, I want my money then." What a break for us. This old pioneer man had been in the country a long time and had run a trading post at Eureka River for years. He had helped many people and had a good name. He and his wife had raised a big family.

The snow was deep. That old 3T D7 didn't have a lot of power and had to push a lot of snow and a big pile of brush too. When the snow melted, the brush was not pushed tight enough together to burn. A lot of hand work had to be done, but when I was finished I had a big field to work on for the summer. I bought a one bottom breaking plow for one hundred dollars. It only cut twenty-four inches at a time, so several hours were spent on a tractor. With steel wheels on the tractor, I was sure not to have a flat tire. Jack pine stumps were hard on the old plow, but with only a 35 Horsepower Case DC4, I couldn't do a lot of damage to the plow.

Sometimes we needed a welder on the spot, so we scratched our dollars together and bought a belt-driven welder from MacLeod's Hardware for one hundred and twenty dollars. I had everything I needed. I fastened it to a big tree to hold it and parked the plow so I could weld on it. Then I parked the tractor so I could put this flat belt onto the pulley on the tractor to drive the welder.

The left front wheel of the old plow kept falling off, so I had done some welding on it. I got down to the far end of the field, turned and started back. I saw a big smoke where the welder was, but by the time I got there, my new welder was burned. Now how was I going to fix the old plow? I just had to cry a little; I couldn't help it.

When the first truckload of grain was harvested off this new field, I was very happy to take the cheque to Mr. Basnett. The whole process had taken two years, clearing it in the winter, breaking, working, picking the roots and stumps off that summer and seeding and harvesting the next year. He was happy to be paid and charged me no interest on the late payment. He was truly a great man to many people.

In the fall of 1964 feed was in, garden put up and winter close at hand. By the time we paid our bills for the summer we had no money left. I heard about the need for a chain saw man to work on a pipeline cleaning project from Willow Flats to Fort Nelson, British Columbia. We talked it over and Rose thought she could manage the cattle with the help of her sister, Shirley.

Four of us rented a little holiday trailer and off we went. Everyone on the job had to supply their own accommodations. Some men lived in tents and some had made a trailer from a pickup box, built a little shell on it and that was home. The work was hard but good. We cut the trees down and had to burn them. We worked two men to a team. With one hundred men and fifty chain saws there was lots of music. The colder it was, the better things burned.

After a week there I asked the foreman if there was any way I could do it without working on Sunday. He looked at me and said, "Man, that's time and a half for you, but if you make a good enough hand and want to work that way, O.K."

It wasn't long until there were extra jobs that needed doing, like going back a few miles, taking some help to clean up some piles that had been missed and several night shifts that needed to be put in on a Cat after a day with a chain saw. Sometimes in the big timber the Cat was used to pile and keep the piles pushed in tight to make them all burn.

One such night, Ken and I were headed for the Cat for a night shift of burning piles. The back wheels fell off the one ton service truck we were driving. What were we going to do now? We knew if we just sat there the day shift wouldn't know what to do, as we had no communication with camp.

We decided that I would go find the Cat, put in a night shift lighting piles and keep them tight while Ken walked back to camp via the pipeline. He would have to walk in the dark with no flashlight and no Cat trail to follow because we had gone out to the Alaska highway, traveled on it for a while, then back into the pipeline. It was sure to be a long hard walk and he would have to get there before day shift left.

He walked into camp just at daybreak, after fifteen miles of tough going, a big river valley to cross and a full day's work the day before. Some young men have a lot of strength and endurance! The mechanic brought the parts for the truck and by noon we had it running. It sure was great to lie down.

One night there was an exiting boxing match on the radio and I spent most of the night out on the Cat because the foreman had become interested in the match. He had forgotten about me until in the middle of the night, then he remembered he was supposed to pick a guy up for supper. He sure was full of apologies.

When we paid our winter's bills for that year, we had twelve hundred dollars left for summer. What a great winter! The rates for that job were two dollars and thirty-five cents per hour for man and saw and we supplied our own room and board.

Chapter Fourteen

Winter Work

Berries were in abundance this year. Rose had canned over two hundred quarts of saskatoons she had picked in the hills and green beans from the garden. We enjoyed every jar!

We were cutting wood and Manny wanted to go help us. We'd made a fire so he could keep warm while we were cutting a load of wood. He'd seen me pour gas in my saw from a gallon jug, so he thought he'd see what would happen if he poured a little on the fire. It didn't take long to find out, a big bang and fire. He slapped the lid back on the gas jug, putting the fire out in it, but my little man's face was badly burned. The doctor said it was only the outside layer and wouldn't leave much scar. He had to eat through a straw for quite awhile for he could hardly open his mouth.

August thirtieth, 1965 was another special day for us as Charles Stanford was born into our family. He was a healthy ten pound ten ounce boy and looked like a little boxer already. Now I had two little boys to teach everything I knew and I was so happy!

Jody had married Brenda Sharon, another great person; and K had married Brenda Karen, a great pioneer girl. She was the daughter of the switch board operator in Hines Creek. When K was a young boy he had inherited the name "Soup", short for Superman that was such a contrast to him. We were quite a crew now. Both Rose and I came from big families, but it was like one big family.

Many good and exiting times took place every year. A lot of time was spent in the saddle with cattle being moved out to grass or home in the fall. There was always a horse that needed training and young men game to do it. All our wives helped their men do whatever they could and down through the years that has built a good relationship.

When we learn to listen; when we can share and let the other one share; when we don't hold grudges; when we don't try to remember the "little things" that were bad; when we don't try to stay mad because it feels good; when we can settle our arguments before we go to sleep; when we make peace before we have to go to work somewhere; when we can be honest with each other; when we can renew our whole commitment to each other and our family; then we can enjoy playing together, praying together, singing together, raising a family together and just being together.

We have tried not to get so mad that we couldn't say, "I'm sorry, forgive me," and "I love you more than yesterday." I heard this line in a song that I appreciate and I have often prayed, "Let me watch my children grow and see what they've become and don't let that cold wind blow till I'm too old to die young."

Christmas was always special as most of the time, Rose would invite all of both our families for supper. It grew to be a house full, but what great times together.

One Christmas Eve, Charlotte andDick wanted Daddy to clean the snow off the dug out with a tractor so they could have a place to skate. In the process, he and the tractor broke through the ice and he nearly drowned. He told us later that as a young man God had been calling him to be a Pastor and he had said, "No, I can't do that, I've never had any training or teaching for that. I'll do anything but be a preacher." When the tractor went down he said, "O.K. Lord, I will do what you want."

In 1966, with the help of a lot of neighbors and friends, and money from friends, we were able to build a new Baptist Church at Worsley which my Dad Pastored for twenty-five years. There grew a great bond between all the different people that worshipped there.

A new road was constructed across the country, now called Highway 64. It saved us lots of miles traveling into Worsley and ran by our homestead. This allowed us to go to town rain or shine.

Electric power was available and we had it installed in our home. We didn't have to run the light plant anymore for lights and there was no more fear of my family being killed from the gas fumes, as had happened once. We now had a phone and TV What a change in our lives.

Mr. Curtis, a blind friend in Hines Creek, would phone when Rose had gone out to feed the cows and do chores. He would talk to each one of the children until they announced, "Mom is back," then he'd hang up knowing all was well for another day. With such a caring spirit from so many people I can say, "It is truly great to be a part of a pioneer era."

We had a lot of acres now with lots of trees on it so my Dad, brothers and I decided we needed to buy a Cat together as a family. We borrowed fifty-five hundred dollars and bought a 3T D7. Our first project was to clear the trees off the right-of-way on the west side of the Clear River, which was to become part of Highway 64. It is great to be a part of history in the making.

We built a big V shaped brush cutter to be pushed by the Cat that would cut trees off at ground level. It worked great. We cleared many acres with this old Cat. We made trails on the lease so the cattle could move and be moved easier.

My brother in law, Keith and I had a lot of good times together. I recall how he would play all kinds of tricks on me. One time when I was courting his sister, I had gotten ready to go home but couldn't, until I discovered I had to remove the blocks from under my car first. But sometimes he had a bad day. One day in particular, he had burned his motorcycle up, so he left the Cat sitting, threw his bike in the bush and took off on a five mile hike to see his Dad who was staying in the cabin out on the lease.

Everyone liked to go visit Grandpa Dixon. Manny was an eight year old and he decided he wanted to ride his little pony up and spend the night with Grandpa. He had learned to operate the swather that summer and cut many acres of hay and I thought if he could swath, he could find the trail to Grandpa's cabin. Well, he did but first he got lost. He took a wrong trail. It was a good thing he left early because it was dark when he arrived and surprised his Grandpa Dick. He and his little pony Teco made many miles together. Four of our children learned to ride on Teco. He was a most popular horse.

Winter rolled around and it was soon time to go to the bush again and look for work for a little money. I went to where a pipeline was being built and inquired about a job for me and my saw. The boss said, "We have our own saws but we are looking for people to run them." I told him I would keep looking until I found a job for me and my saw. He thought about it then said, "If you can burn those two big piles of green poplar, you've got a job."

By mid afternoon I had two big smokes going. I knew that by getting up on top of the pile, bucking up a lot of sticks until there was a big hole, then getting a dry tree, starting a fire with that, then putting the green ones on top, it wouldn't be long until I would have to get out of there, because the fire goes right to the bottom. I had a job with that company until the project was finished.

In 1967, my bother, Blue knew something was happening to him. After much testing, the specialits discovered a tumor in the back of his brain and told him they would have to operate to remove it. They advised him, he should make sure he had his will in order, because at that time the success rate of an operation like that was twenty-five percent in his favor. Without the operation he would continue to deteriorate. That was a tough decision for him. He was not even thirty years old and had a young family. He felt he had no choice but to go through with the operation.

The doctor told him his heart had quit beating twice during the operation but it was a success. They had removed the tumor through a hole they had drilled in the back of his skull. His time was not up yet. In 1968 he and his family moved to Canada to make Worsley their home too. He sure had mellowed out since he was a boy.

Winter was soon here again and this time Blue, Jody and I went looking for work. We found our winter's work in the Rainbow Lake area. This turned out to be a contract job in two areas. The banker informed me that I could borrow up to three thousand dollars at the bank.

We finished the first job, but were having trouble finding the second one. A Cat had plowed a trail up to where we needed to go. We had started on December 3 and the snow was getting quite deep. The man with the contract supplied us with a Bombardier to travel with. Our transportation broke down about ten miles from camp one night. Blue was pretty weak yet and there was no way out but to walk. He laid down in the trail and said he couldn't make it, but after a rest, he got up and went again.

It was late when we got to the trailer where we stayed. Blue announced he would not do that again for a thousand dollars! The next day our snow mobile broke down two miles further away from camp and he walked it again, for free.

When we finished the job we found out our boss was bankrupt. Our banker then was a good man and helped us, so we were able to get our money direct from the oil company. That put us in touch with a man who represented Northern Geophysical. It turned out that this company had a lot of miles left from the previous winter that needed slashing. Since we were already there and willing, we had lots of work ahead of us. We spent the next three weeks living in a tent and working with snow mobiles.

My brother-in-law, Keith was already working with us but now we needed more help. We had lots of young friends that were game to take on this type of experience.

We loaded the two snow mobiles and sleds with eight people, their gear, two tents, an oil heater for one tent and a small wood heater for the other. This little heater was to be our cook stove also. Our camp was about thirty miles away from the plowed in trail. The boys said, "It's going to be pretty wintery in our tent, the tank for the oil heater has a big hole in it."

When you are gone all day away from your tent in winter everything is like a rock when you get back, so we made some provisions. Rose had broken about a dozen eggs in each plastic bag and boiled a lot of potatoes. We had a lot of togetherness at night but usually within an hour, everyone was fed and stories of the day were in high gear. We learned that if we filled our water pail with snow on top of the water, our pail wouldn't break and we could get water right away.

It was between twenty five and forty below zero for those three weeks. I was amazed at how a body could adapt to the cold. Almost every night someone would freeze out of the other tent and come in and make a fire in ours. With a fire going it was great, but when the fire went out there was no difference in the inside or outside temperature.

Four man tents don't have much extra room when four men are stretched out sleeping. One night Keith froze out and came in, put wood in the stove, poured in some power saw gas and dropped a match in and bang! A man from Czechoslovakia was sleeping with his head about six inches from the front of the stove and instantly his long, curly black hair was aflame. To be wakened from a sound sleep with someone hitting you on the head created a great stir; suddenly several referees were needed.

Blue had gone to find the next place we were moving to. Some new Cats had moved in and were opening up some new lines. He stopped the pickup to see if he could hear the Cats. He had bounced the battery out of place so the pickup wouldn't start.

He started walking and came to the line where we would be traveling back to our trailer. He built a fire and waited for us to come along. Meanwhile, a truck came along and offered him a ride, so he jumped in with him. A few miles down the trail they rolled the truck on a corner. Blue was on the bottom and with some difficulty, he managed to crawl out of the window and started walking again. Another truck came by and gave him a ride into Rainbow Lake. There he rented a truck and went out to the camp where our trailer was.

We had finished our project about dark and went to our tents. The boys wanted to load up and go to the trailer so we did. I have been amazed at what a double track Skidoo can pull. We loaded our entire camp on the toboggans; the guys gave a push and we were off. We had several bad hills in front of us, thirty miles to go and it was already 9:30 p.m. by the time we got all loaded up. The guys all pushed when we came to a hill.

When we came to the place where Blue had made the fire, we couldn't figure out what that was all about. We pulled into camp about 1:30 a.m. hungry but too tired to cook. Blue was sitting at the table. We asked him what he was doing just sitting at the table at this time of night and he said, "If a man lives through the kind of day I just had, he should just sit down and be thankful he's still alive!"

We hadn't had any of our work checked yet by the forestry. The forestry department needed to inspect our work, then they would give approval to the oil company so we could be paid for the job. It was turning colder. After a couple of days and still no inspectors, we went to a phone and found that they wouldn't fly until it was warmer. We talked to a friend that said he would come and inspect it if he had a snow mobile to ride, even if it was cold.

At the far end of the job one of the pulleys broke on the machine he was riding. We took the skis off, turned them around and set the back of it on the back of the double track snow mobile I was riding. He climbed on the seat and away we went. It would have made quite a picture. We had to unhook several times, tip the double track over and poke the snow out. I have never seen the snow do that before or since. It would pack in between the tracks, pushing the top of the tracks up and they'd get so tight, they couldn't turn.

We were getting close to completing the inspection and the inspector had run out of cigarettes. He said, "When we get back to the truck, I'm going to smoke four cigarettes before I even help you load the machines." The next morning all the boys were curious if the job had passed or not, as everyone was being paid by the mile.

He looked at them real cool and said, "Boys, I hate to tell you but it's not good enough." Well, what a sad looking crew, they could visualize living in the freezing tents. After breakfast he said, "No, boys, that was an excellent job." Then there was more joy than at Christmas time.

We did one more job before break-up but snow had gotten so deep the snow mobiles couldn't go in the deep, powdery snow, so we rented a Bombardier to make trails.

Blue's truck was in bad shape. He had hit a bridge and knocked the rear end completely out of it and on one of the trips home after one hundred miles at thirty m.p.h., he lost his cool and with his boot put a big dent in the dash. This dent remained as long as he owned that truck.

It was May 5 before our money for that job came through. What a relief for all the crews, their families and the Royal Bank.

Keith was back to good health after his big feed of orange ice cream and then a cigar. He had recently gotten married, so he thought he should be able to handle a cigar and maybe he could have if he hadn't inhaled. But this was one time in his life that he couldn't laugh at something funny.

We had come across a car that was way off the road in the snow. We stopped to see if they were all right. A man got out and walked to the end of the car, holding on to it and said, "I'm drunk." He took one more step and did a nose dive in the deep snow. After a few seconds he rose up completely covered in snow and said, "Now, do you believe I'm drunk?" He had lots of gas and the temperature outside was warm. He said he wanted to sleep and I thought that was the best place for him. At lease he wouldn't run into anyone. Keith was mad because he couldn't even laugh; he was so sick. The next stop we made, he lost all his ice cream. He felt better after that and could actually laugh again.

That winter we had more than we could do and had to hire more help.

It's been said that behind every good man there's a great woman. The Hale boys sure had good mates. This winter work had put more responsibility on our wives. But everything was "ours," not "this is mine and that's yours."

Jerry Sideroff had come to work for us. One hot day on our homestead, he was looking for a drink and saw a jug in the back of our pickup. Presuming it was water, he took a big slug before he realized it was bleach. He thought he was going to die but he was tough. He stayed and worked with us for several years. We nicknamed him Sid.

Our winter work was together but we each had our own farms and cattle. The winter work sure helped us lots. One time I fell through the ice on a river with my new pickup. We pulled it out and left it by the river. Then I went on a snow mobile eighty-five miles to deliver some maps to another crew. When I got back to my truck, I found that all the brakes and the starter were frozen. I had to take the starter off and thaw it out to get it going. I was more careful of ice and pickups after that.

It was in this area that Blue, Jody, Sid and I had to spend the night by the fire once. One of our Skidoos broke down and we concluded that we'd spend the night and work our way back to the truck the next day. It was either that or spend half the night getting back to our camp and turning around and repeating it next morning. A sandwich lunch had to carry us until the next night when we'd be back in camp.

So with lots of spruce boughs on the ground, no blankets, and a big fire, we were there until day break. It was cold and we could only lay a little while, then the side away from the fire got cold. When you are dressed for working, you are really not dressed for sleeping around a camp fire. It took lots of wood and when day break came, we were out cutting trees as there was no meal to prepare or coffee to brew.

There were four big coulees to cross. I could pull the broken machine with my machine on level ground but at the bottom of each hill, I had to unhook, drive to the top of the hill, take the drive pulley off, walk back down, put it on the other machine and take it to the top of the hill. It took most of my time getting this crippled machine out. We were at camp shortly after dark and a big supper was on the menu.

The next two winters were in the Fort Nelson area. I was at home for a few days when one day the phone rang. Blue said, "We need another machine up here, ours is broke down at the bottom of the Fort Nelson River Valley." He and Jody were finishing a job and living in a tent. When their machine broke down, they had walked back to camp. It was thirty below zero. They had taken the battery out of the truck and into the tent beside the wood heater and warmed it up. They hoped the pickup would start as they only had one and were a hundred miles east of the highway.

After Blue phoned they headed back to their suite and were still asleep when Rose and I pulled in the next morning. She had come along to help me drive.

There was only a day's work left on that job so we went out to finish it. About mid afternoon we missed Jody. We stopped our chain saws and then we could hear his saw idling back over behind the brush pile. There he was, stretched out on the snow. We threw some snow in his face and he sat up, looked around and said, "What happened?" A tree had knocked him out but he was all right.

With a bit of wire we were able to get the crippled Skidoo back to camp. Rose had supper made and camp all ready to load so we loaded up and headed down the trail shortly after dark.

Jody was always playing tricks on someone. One day he had broken the chain on his saw and was heading for the pickup to get another when he noticed one of the guys cutting in a very high tension place. With trees bent around each other they do some funny things sometimes when you cut them so you have to be very careful to be sure you are on the right side of the tree when you cut it. Jody walked up behind the guy, unbeknownst to him, stuck his chain saw between his legs and revved up his saw. Poor Norm just kind of floated up about two feet. There was almost a murder case that day.

Shortly after that, we had to shut down for a few days to help get one of the crew members married on February 14. Victor had been with us on a lot of jobs and now he had a wife to support.

That winter we had slashed just over twelve hundred miles and that made a big winter for us. We had one unfinished job to go do the next spring. So Norm, Mildred, Rose and I loaded two horses, a dog and our gear in our truck and headed back to Fort Nelson. We had a thirty mile journey back in the bush on foot with the horses packing our gear, saws, etc., to where the work was.

The creeks were high in June and we had to fall trees across them to carry our supplies across, then pack up again. Rose had rigged up our old dog Rover to pack such things as sardines and canned milk and he crossed the creeks on the logs just like a pro. After persuading the horses they could swim if we pulled on the rope, they did fine too. The muskegs were high and the water was cold. The wild roses were loaded with flowers. What a honeymoon!

" One time I was getting ready to go do a job and Manny said, "I'll go with you, ride Teco and carry gas and oil for you, I'm ten now you know." He was quite a little cowboy now. It was only a small job we had to do so, that's what he did. We were getting low on chain saw oil one time so we sent him back to the truck for more. The river had risen since we had crossed in the morning but into the water he and Teco went. The current was stronger than before and took them downstream. He said he grabbed a limb and climbed out and Teco was right behind him. He got the oil and had to cross this creek again to get back. They made it safely and Manny has memories for life.

Later on, he and his uncle, Ken had their three wheeler upside down in a creek with a strong current. They almost became history that time.

Soup and Sid were blown out of their trailer one night. They had a small leak in the propane line underneath the trailer. The fumes could not escape because they had the trailer banked with snow.

When they went to light their stove, there was a loud bang and out they went through the door. Another miracle they weren't both killed. To be miles from anywhere some ordeals like that could have been very serious but they were able to repair the damage and finish the job.

Author at living quarters for winter brushwork, 1971

"Moving to another job"

Chapter Fifteen
Our Home in Cleardale

The time had come to buy our own place and move off the Sherley land which K and Brenda would move onto.

In 1970 a half section came up for sale in Cleardale, twenty-five miles west of us. There were enough acres cleared on it to qualify for title and we knew there was more land surrounding it that would be coming up for sale.

We took Dick and Florence along with us for a ride to look at the new place with us. Florence was holding her jaw and groaning a bit. I finally asked her what her problem was. She said, "My tooth is killing me"! I asked her if she wanted me to pull it and she said, "Yes,, stop the truck"! I did and we all got out. I took my pliers off the dash of the pickup, and wiped them clean on my pants. She walked over to some green grass and took her coat off. She laid her coat on the grass then she laid down on her coat and opened her mouth. She pointed to one of her jaw teeth and said, "That one". What had I got myself into, I couldn't chicken out now, she was so brave. I said, "Rose, you hold her forehead down, it's going to be a tough pull". It was. She sat up, spit a little blood and said, "Oh, boy, that feels better"! We got back in the pickup and carried on, no more toothache.

Rose and I talked it over and decided to take our horses and go have a look to see if the river hills adjoining this land would have any good grazig for cattle. After spending the day riding and looking, we decided this would be a real challenge for us and would make a good ranch someday.

It was mostly covered with poplar trees. I was thirty, my partner twenty eight and we had children that were big enough to be a lot of help already, so we borrowed the money and bought six quarters of land.

The next summer we bought two more quarters and the following year two more. We knew we had four quarters that we didn't owe anything on but they were too far away for us to farm now. We decided to sell them and pay down on this new debt.

After nine years of being on a calf crop share, getting our homestead cleared and broke and roots all picked, plus another bush quarter and a part bush covered quarter cleared and in cultivation, there had been many experiences for two kids.

I was twenty one when we started the calf crop sharing. It had meant working in the bush in the winter and fencing, haying and clearing more land every year. We found down through the years that the Lord sure had been good to His children.

We knew there were many things that had to be done to build a ranch. First we needed a house. We both wanted a log one so in February we got a permit and fell seventy straight Jack Pine trees and skidded them into a pile so a log truck could haul them to our building site.

My father in law helped us pick the building logs that came off Ike's Hill west of Worsley. Now I knew that come spring we had a log house to build. We got the trees when the sap was down to minimize shrinkage.

Winter was passing fast and I needed to go check on the crews and take supplies. We were slashing in four different areas, as well as trying to keep four skidders going, plus fallers and landing men. It seemed like I needed to be in several places at once. It was good to see the snow go and the mud come. This meant we were finished for another winter.

When I got home Rose had a big fresh bouquet of crocuses on the table. They were always the first flower to bloom in the spring.

She had the cows mostly all calved out and had lost very few calves. The grass on the hills was starting to come and the cows could soon go out to graze. We knew it would be our last winter and spring here in this place we had enjoyed so much but we were looking forward to being at our own place!

That spring we had extra crop to seed with the old place and the new one. By mid June we had the crops in, the fences mended that the moose had broken in the winter, and the logs for the new house peeled and covered so the rain wouldn't stain them.

We chose the spot we wanted to build on and staked the area for the basement to be dug. The Cat operator had dug the hole for the basement four feet too deep before I caught him so we had to move over and dig another one.

We made a cement foundation for an old building we planned to use for a shop. When we started to move the building it collapsed, so we burned it and built a new one.

We had the forms up for the basement, gravel and cement ready and were waiting for the mixer truck operator to come. He came in the evening and said, "I have to have this truck back in town by 8:00 a.m. it's now or wait till I come back." We worked all night pouring all the cement for the basement walls and finished up just as Rose had breakfast ready.

I only found one guy that said he knew how to make dove tailed corners. He said he'd come and help us get started. Nick stayed with me until the last log was up.

We were wanting to build without a debt so that meant I had to go back to the bush again. This time I took my 350 JD crawler with a six way blade to put in erosion ditches. Grandpa Dick was going to take a horse to do the grass seeding. When night came, that's where we camped. This was in the Grand Cache area.

Once crossing a slough in between two hills, I got part way across and realized I was in trouble. There was a big hole in the moss that had burned several years before. The whole area around me was shaking. I looked back to stop Grandpa but he was already bogged down with the horse. I didn't think I could stop and back out, but soon I had to stop. There was no place to go with two big holes in front. The front of the Cat started dropping fast. I shut the Cat off and went to help Grandpa get the horse out. I thought I'd never get the Cat out of this one. It was the eleventh time we had been stuck on this job and were almost finished.

With a tree as big as we could carry, we tied it to the rail on the back. The front was now a foot deeper than when I left it. What a relief when it crawled out on the log. I didn't have to leave it there after all!

I was a happy guy, with the roof on the house, bush work done, three hundred acres broke and worked down and the move almost made.

Since I didn't get to finish high school, when an opportunity came along to learn something new I tried to learn it and now was my chance to learn to fly an airplane. It was a night course for the ground school. The bush work was organized and going so I took the chance and laid down the seven hundred dollars.

Before I had completed the lessons my friend Frank says, "Maybe we should buy a plane together." So we went shopping and found a 1956 Cessna 170 with five hundred and twenty hours total time on it. This plane, ZPI, Zulu Papa India, saved a lot of hours driving to look at jobs.

One day Rose and I were on our way to Calgary in ZPI when our radio quit. When we hit the control zone I wondered, "Now, what are we going to do, we can't stay up here all night!"

The Industrial Airport is a big busy place for a plane with no radio. We buzzed the tower, lined up with the active run way when it was clear, and got a green light! That was great to see!

It was getting cold so we moved into our new log home. We had to set things on the floor as we had no cupboards built yet. When I turned on the propane furnace, I thought of all the wood cutting days.

Sometimes neighbors would lend each other a hand to saw up the wood supply. A big pile of trees would be stacked ready to saw into stove lengths and water would be warmed and poured into the radiator. A buzz saw with a big blade on it was used. The blocks would fly and a wood pile was in the making. By the end of the day there would be a tired crew and the next day they'd move to someone else's place.

The women got together and fed the men, just like Christmas dinners. Everyone was glad to look out and see their big wood piles. Since the chain saws, that part of history is gone.

We had finished working for the winter when Dick Mercer, a boss for one of the seismic companies, caught me and said he really needed me to do one more job. He said we could stay in their main camp and they'd fly us back and forth to work. Well, he had been so fair to me through the years, that it was hard to turn him down. I told him my Jeep was sick, it badly needed a head gasket and U joint.

We had to cross the Nelson, Liard, Beaver, and the Crow Rivers all on the ice. It was already getting muddy in places. We spun out on a hill with the Jeep loaded on a trailer we were pulling. We were still using a two wheel drive pickup. We slid back and tipped the Jeep off. We had to leave it there until a head gasket was flown in to camp.

Tin oil cans have a lot of uses. The new U joint was the wrong one. We took it apart and found all the bearings were gone. We cut a long strip of tin from an oil can and wrapped it around the cross bars where the needle bearings were missing. Then, we packed it full of grease and had no more trouble.

After the tenth shift with a 7F Cat they had made a trail up to Scatter Mountain.

The main camp was full one night. The chopper never came for us so down the trail to this new Cat camp we went for the night. The Cat camp was a bunk house on a big sleigh that the Cat moved every few days, to be closer to their work.

The hill was slick with a corner at the bottom of it. When we arrived, the main bunk house was on it's side with the night shift trying to sleep inside. The water barrel strapped to the wall that was kept full with snow water was now empty. The diesel heater was spilling diesel out of it. The cook and crew climbed out, onto the Jeep and onto the ground. Here we were with no movie camera.

We got the camp back on the sleigh and parked for the night. The cook wasn't very happy. We told him we had a real need of a place to lie down and we sure would be gateful if we had a little food. We were trying to use all the tact we had because we were quite needy.

Then the light plant quit. He said, "If you get me some water and lights, I can feed you and you can sleep on the floor, but we have no blankets." The barrel was soon full of clean snow to melt for water. With some cap wire hooked to a spare battery from the Cat and a spare light from the Cat hung from the ceiling, we soon had lights also. It was a whole lot better than a bed of spruce boughs on the snow and nothing to put in our stomachs!

With chains on all four tires, we still spun out climbing back up the hill the next day, so we hooked a long cable from the winch to a tree and up we went.

A different chopper came to pick us up that night. As we dropped off the mountain, we normally followed a valley to camp but this time the new pilot was following the mountain around. It was snowing heavy and the only way you could see was down. I thought we were going in the wrong direction so I leaned ahead and suggested this to the pilot. He said, "I'm flying this thing."

I watched my watch and his compass and after six minutes of nothing but trees below he turned and said, "Where do you think camp is?" I suggested a one eighty degree turn and twelve minutes later camp was just below us. I breathed a "Thank you again, Lord." The pilot said not a word as we got out and away he went to pick up some more men.

We finished on April 18, 1970. When we got to the Beaver River, the Cat camp had parked for the night, it didn't look good. Lots of water was running under the fill they'd made of logs and snow. We would have been out a day sooner but one of the Cat skinners read his map wrong and cut a line in the wrong direction. We had to do that line for free I might add, as we were on a contract.

We told them, "If we break through, tell our family what happened, we are going home." The Nelson had a hole in the ice big enough that the front tires were just wide enough to clear it. At home the fields were dry so there was no rest time that year.

Some jobs were good and some were tough. Danny and Kerry had phoned looking for work. I told them, "I have a tough job to do. We'll have to get into the job with snow mobiles and live in a tent." They said, "We are young, tough and need the work. We can do it."

As soon as they arrived, we got our gear all together and headed for Fort Nelson, British Columbia. We hired a plane on skis to haul one skidoo and all of our gear to be dropped off at the Beaver River Airstrip. From the Beaver Airstrip, we were two days getting to where home was going to be for the next few days.

Everything had to be burned back a quarter mile from a pipeline crossing. Digging it out of the snow made things difficult. Five days later we were back on the goose headed for Fort Nelson. We knew the next one would be tougher as we had farther to go with snow machines.

Arrangements were made with the Forestry Department. They informed us of the date they would be doing an inspection and would also bring us a ten gallon drum of gas.

The snow was deep and it hadn't been very cold. When we got to the Nelson it was dark. Checking and finding there was open water above the crossing; we elected to camp for the night. If you have ever tried using alder to cook or heat with, you know how much fun it is and how big a pile of ashes you have by morning.

We loaded up and decided if we hit the river full speed with two inches of ice at the crossing, we could make it. It was like climbing a hill going across on the other side. We had thirty miles left to go. The next morning we were burning trees early. There was much more work to do here than we'd anticipated and we were running short of food. Danny turned twenty one so Kerry and I talked it over and decided we could spare him an extra slice of bread for his birthday.

The chopper was two days overdue. Our saws were out of gas and we had one hundred and fifty feet left to cut and burn. To make matters worse we were out of supplies. The boys had a plan. We could drain the gas from one skidoo and put it in the other. They could make it at least half way to the pickup and walk the rest of the way. They could get some gas and groceries and be back the next afternoon.

About 5:00 a.m. I heard a noise. I couldn't figure out what it was for about fifteen minutes then I realized it was a skidoo. By the time they got there I had the fire going.

What a story they related. First a tree knocked their light out. Then one ski had run under a tree and broke off. They had to ride it like a bike after that. So here was two guys on it dragging a barrel along behind in the dark. They had a real challenge. But they had made it all the way to the pickup on half a tank of fuel, filled the barrel, filled the machine and made it back on one ski. It was one hundred and sixty miles to make the round trip.

After a two hour sleep we loaded up and headed out. Just before we got to the Fort Nelson River, the helicopter flew over. He stopped and left the ten gallons of gas, then away he went.

When we got into town, I phoned the Forest Ranger and the first thing he asked was, when I was going back to finish the last one. I told him, "Man, if it isn't good enough, I'll never be back!" That work was all done for no pay.

There are some wonderful people in government and some must have paid to get their jobs. One inspector told me one day that I had to climb up and tie a winch line on to a certain tree and pull it down. It had balanced in a fork about thirty feet off the ground after it had been cut. A good strong wind would bring it down.

The reason for bucking all these trees was so they would lay flat, and this would increase the rotting rate and prevent the travel of fires down these piles. It has worked. Also the erosion prevention has helped as there was a great deal of erosion happening before.

One such man made an oil company bring a back hoe in three times to clean out one creek crossing. I had a job finished in his area and he looked at it and said everything was good except one erosion ditch that was causing a lot of problems. After the third time in with my machine, it still wasn't good enough. I suggested the only thing left to do was for him to get his boss, I'd get the one that signed my cheque and the four of us would have a look at it. I knew the erosion ditch came from a few miles away at an old airstrip and this Cat line happened to cross this ditch. He volunteered to have another look and this time it was O.K.

Every summer we had land to break and roots, stumps and piles to clean up. Now that we had a root rake with seven big wheels with teeth on them changed the whole aspect of new land. One of my neighbors said he felt like just getting off and kissing the thing every round he made, it saved so much work. Since we had started logging in the winter with a skidder and putting a piler blade on it in the summer, it was much easier to burn the root rows and brush piles.

One of my friends told me one day that he had a brand new skidder. He said he'd like me to take it and pay him as I could. What trust! Al has helped me out a lot of times. Some of the skidders that I had in the past required more time working on them than they worked.

One night I had been working on a skidder and on my way down this long hill, my lights went out on my little Jeep. There was a corner at the bottom of the hill and over I went. I knew Blue and Jody were coming back out and I had a warm coat and was tired so I laid down in front of the Jeep and went to sleep. The next thing I knew Blue was pounding on me and hollering, "Are you alive?" I guess it did look kind of bad. It had snowed a bit and here's a guy lying on the ground with fresh snow on him, beside a vehicle on its side. I had to promise I'd never do that again before they'd give me a ride.

In August 1972, a man at the other end of the phone said, "Can you take a crew and cut a road way up to the top of Bowser Mountain, so we can put a big rig up on there to drill a hole?" Two days later we arrived at the Bell Irving River where a camp was being set up just beside the beautiful Cassiar Highway.

We were several days ahead of the Cats building the road and the boss decided we should go to the airstrip where the Meziadin runs into the Nass and extend it. We found it was a great place to fish. One day Cornie and I went to catch a fish. I caught one right away. I told Cornie, "You have to walk down river a bit and cast to the edge of the clear water."

He is a big man and had on a big coat. The rocks were slick and he didn't want to fall down in the cold water. As I pulled the first one I caught past him I'd asked him to reach down and pick it up, he was part way in the river. He got hold of the line, lifted, one flop and the line broke. Away went my fish. I put on another hook and went in for his brother. This time I pulled a nice Coho right past him over to the shore.

When Cornie saw this away he went to the good place. Sure enough, bingo. He had on light line, a small reel and a big Coho on the other end! It took a lot of cranking and he was making good headway. Down he went on the slick rocks. I thought he was going into the Nass but before I could get to him he was up, rod high in the air, and soaking wet. After the little reel wouldn't do any more, he wrapped the line around his hand and a big Coho salmon went to shore. The cook back at camp froze them for us and they made for some good feasts.

Back in the bunk house one night we found out one of the guys was a champion squaw wrestler. I told him I was too and the contest was on. Soon we were both lying on our backs with our right legs hooked. One of the guys put his foot on my left foot and I flipped the champ right over! I never told Danny for a long time that it hadn't been a fair match.

The only markers we had to follow were ribbons dropped from a chopper. The terrain was very rough and we had to use our own judgment sometimes to make slight changes. One day I was knocked down three times. Hard hats were sure a life saver there.

Our job was to fall the trees and burn the brush for the right of way to the top of the mountain. The trees were skidded into a pile to be hauled away. A big percentage of the trees were over mature, with only a ring around the outside of the trees that was any good. The inside was rotten. It was impossible to fall these trees in the direction that we wanted them to go.

When we finished with the falling, piling and burning, the Cats were building a road so an oil rig could be hauled up to the top of the mountain.

The year before, this oil company had brought in a bull dozer, took it all apart and flown it up to the top of the mountain with a chopper. Then, they had put it back together again to build a place for an oil rig to sit. They had taken apart and flown the rig to the top as well. They found that rig was too small and decided they wanted a bigger one up there so they could drill deeper.

It was a good crew to work with. Our foreman, Bill Thompkins was a neighbor. He had recommended me so I felt like we needed to do a good job for him.

We finished the clearing job the day after the first snow. They wanted me to stay and build a big log building to store the mud in that they used for drilling. This was a snow belt, so a building with a strong roof was needed to hold all the deep snow there. I couldn't stay any longer as I knew it was well into harvest time and I was anxious to get home.

Manny was a big help now. He was twelve that year. He had started operating the swather when he was eight and now he was quite a little man with lots of experience. He made Rose a good helper.

The hay crop had been heavy and Rose and Manny had borrowed a hay haybine from a neighbor, as the haying weather wasn't too great. A hay haybine will cut a heavy crop. It mashes the stems as they are going through so it will dry faster. Then it puts it in a wind row out of the back. They had the haying done, with thanks to our good neighbor, Kenny Hoover for lending them the hay haybine. We had a good crop that year. Lots of it was a first crop on new land so there were still lots of sticks and roots on the ground.

By the time I got home a heavy, wet snow had fallen. As I stood looking out across the field where the beautiful wheat and canola was growing, I just couldn t keep all the tears back. It had looked so promising and now it was all flat.

I knew all the expense for the summer meant I would have to leave my home and family again and go back to the bush with my chain saw to make some needed money.

The next spring we were able to salvage most of our wheat but the canola had to be burned off. Being as it was on new land and had so many roots, it was impossible to pick up, even with long fingers on the reel that were built just for that purpose.

One day I was riding a little Appaloosa mare and was going to get a tire for my one ton, which I had left laying on the edge of the field. I had the rope tied onto the tire ready to pull home. The tire moved one inch and it felt like dynamite exploded under me. After it seemed like an hour of the pounding and abuse I was taking, she stopped. The bridle was off her head and the bits were pulled up against her chest. How all this happened is an unsolvable mystery. The bad part was I had experienced such a wild ride, with not one witness present!

Our home in Cleardale

86

Chapter Sixteen
Great Rewards

In the summer of 1973 we took the phone off the hook and headed for Alaska. With our family of four, our nephew, Harvey Lubeck, a friend, Jake Fehr and a crew cab with a canopy on it, we were off.

My brother, K and his wife Brenda were pastoring a Baptist church in Terrace, B.C. then. We visited them and their two daughters, Toni and Holly for a day or two.

Then we headed up the lava bed road to the Stewart Cassiar Highway. It seemed that every stream had fish in it and we thought the scenery was gorgeous.

We camped out every night and each one had their tasks to do. With seven people there is a lot of camping gear.

We thought Tatogga Lake was especially attractive with the mountains on both sides.

Many of the lakes and streams were full of delicious rainbow trout. I thought what a fly fishermen paradise with wild rainbow trout!

We spent a day in the museum at Dawson City and toured the old abandoned dredges. That kind of thing always interested me. We all enjoyed the trip with the beautiful scenery, but were glad to be back home.

Teco was Stan's horse now. Manny, Darla and Lisa had all learned to ride on him and had progressed to bigger horses. Stan, Teco and old Rover spent a lot of hours together. Stan used to ride Teco backwards a lot of times just to show what a great trick horse he was. Wherever Stan was, usually old Rover was there too sometimes on leash, sometimes just there.

From the time our daughters were young they were lots of help and full of fun and laughter. One exception to their happy times was in the middle of the night in calving time if there was a cold wind blowing and it was their turn to go check the cows. If there was a cow in trouble, then they grumbled a bit.

They learned how to milk the cow and how to plant and care for the garden. At a young age they could cook a great meal or ride a horse to help move the cattle. They were good machine operators. Our girls would usually listen to instructions and try to follow them. Most of the time boys just want to see how fast it will go.

One day Rose wanted to help on the granary we were starting to put together. She instructed her girls what she expected them to have done for the day. She also told them we would be coming in to dine at noon on the dot and we would be wanting fried chicken. This meant they had to go out to the hen house and catch one, kill, pluck, butcher and cook it. She also ordered a plain cake with custard poured over top of it for dessert.

Well, when lunch time came they had everything all ready. Everything looked wonderful. The table was set and everybody was happy. We sat down and enjoyed a nice meal, but it would have been nicer if they had taken all the insides from the chicken first. Rose always believed a child learned best by doing.

One of the guys that was helping us one fall had a problem with bad smelly feet. One day at lunch time one of our daughters slipped away from the table. She soon came back with a can of spray deodorant and under the table she went and gave his feet a good spraying. They had seen their mother have fun so they practiced having fun too.

One day Rose rigged up a plastic spider to a thread and hung it high bove Jake's plate and when he sat down and started filling his plate, she went over to the kitchen sink and tripped the spider loose. When it hit in Jake's plate the expression was worth a thousand laughs. If we can't find a little laughter in everyday life, it can be tough on us and our life style had room for lots of laughs.

Darla and Lisa are wonderful daughters. They were always fun to be with and turned out to be great cooks. When it came to field work, they were great helpers There were many days of root picking by hand and burning root piles. There were many days my little daughters worked for a while to get all the dirt off themselves. No matter how tough the job, if I could convince them it needed doing, they were willing workers. There just weren't many tasks that they wouldn't tackle. Daughters have a way of getting into their Dad's heart. I know our daughters are so like their mother in lots of ways. It was very important that we teach our girls everything we could so they would become good wives and mothers someday.

Our new neighbor, Bert said, "Let's get a sawmill and edger and make some lumber." So I got out the logs and he was the millwright. We had lumber for ourselves and sold some.

One night Bert called over and asked for some help, one of his yearlings had gotten out. It was dark and the calf had to go through the barn to get back into its pen.

They had an old ram sheep that was getting pretty mean. His wife, Kay had forgotten about the ram when she ran into the barn to turn on the light. Wham, he sent her flying. After the fight, she came back out. The light was on and she was pretty upset. She made sure that the ram didn't die from old age.

My sister, Charlotte had met this guy from Ontario that was working on a survey crew. Being the only girl with five brothers, it was a big job for Bruce to win everyone's approval. It seemed like he might be all right.

On their wedding day, we wanted Bruce to get off to a clean start so with the help of a neighbor or two, he was thrown into the dugout. Now he was initiated into the family. We have shared many good times together, playing, hunting, neighboring and worshipping the same Lord.

Bruce was kind of slow sometimes and it took him an hour and a half to land a forty three pound salmon in the wild Skeena one time. It might have had something to do with the mini rod and reel he was using. As soon as he had the salmon on shore, the rod broke in two. For many years Bruce and Charlotte were our closest neighbors and we enjoyed many happy times together.

While on the Menno Simons School Board, I became aware that there was a thirteen year old boy that needed a home, so we took him to live with us for five years. Mark was energetic and eager to learn. He became a good power saw and machinery operator.

At that point in time, we had five teenagers which makes for lots of fun in different forms. When it came meal time, it took a lot of food to feed everyone.

Rose's youngest brother, Jim spent some time with us. One morning I had called downstairs many times for him and Dave to get up and at it, but there was no response. I hadn't realized how tough Jim had grown to be until I took my new stock prod and held it about an inch from his big toe. I pressed the button and the blue sparks flew. He never even wiggled.

Jim's brothers, Ken and Keith had warned him that if he quit school or failed they were going to give him a licking. He didn't take them serious until the day came, then it was quite a round! I think he thought it would probably have been better to stay and work harder in school.

One day, our friends Carl and Ruth, seen something laying on the road and stopped to see what it was. There was a piston and farther on down the road laid the connecting rod for my pickup. Rose's oldest sister, Flossie is a mute and had married Dave, who is also mute. Dave was working for us at the time. He thought he was in high gear but with a three speed shift on the steering column, he didn't know for sure. When a truck is in first gear and you want to go the speed limit, it can't take the revs forever, so there it sat.

It was kind of a sad day when the papers were signed to sell our homestead. Out of the three hundred and twenty acres on it we had two hundred and ninety cleared, broke and most of the roots picked. We had planned to put the money on the debt for the new land and that's what we did.

After selling my share of ZPI I felt really lost without it. We still needed a plane. Even with good horses and pickups, I still couldn't be every where I needed to be. Our work now was scattered over Northern Alberta and North East B.C. Rose and I decided if we had our own plane, it would mean a lot less travelling for me, I could be home more with my family and a used plane probably wouldn't cost much more than a pickup. We had a good crop that year so I borrowed part of the money and went looking for one.

I found a 172 Cessna CYR in Manitoba. The owner agreed to fly it to Peace River for me. He ran into lots of rain in flight.

By the time I had it registered and checked over, the weather had turned cold so when I flew it home the air speed indicator didn't work. It had gotten water in the little tube and frozen. Since air speed is pretty important in take off and landings, I was a bit nervous. I thought, "The first airplanes didn't have an air speed indicator." So I flew it that way until I got comfortable with no air speed indicator then I thawed it out.

One very warm day, with four people on board and full of fuel I took off to go check out a job. There was a power line at the end of the runway. That day heavily loaded, the stall horn that buzzed 5 mph before nose down, was buzzing like crazy. We just cleared the power line! There was an angel that gave us a little lift. It was just too close and the power line got buried after that.

Four years later, I thought the bush work was over for me. We didn't owe anything on our land or buildings. We sold the plane and bought more cows.

As we had more new land to seed every year we needed more grain storage, so every summer there was a new building to be erected. There were also more fences to build and cattle sheds, etc. When your family is healthy and happy it is a great joy doing things together. We felt like the Lord was very good to us indeed. We had lots of bush jobs in the winter and the farm was a good place to spend the money in the summer! We were growing good crops and able to have jobs for several men in the winter and summer.

One year it had started to rain in July and continued until our crop was dead ripe and the heads began to fall off onto the ground. I built a long iron push pole and with a tractor pushing a combine, I was able to pick up most of the crop; it didn't all fall to the ground. There were many endurance tests.

We now had four Skidders which took a pretty big crew of men. These men had to be very capable too, as there was a lot of hand falling, limbing and topping with chain saws. The slashing camps were always moving from one job to the next one. It was always good when I could give someone a break on the Skidder or take a saw and go to one of the slashing crews and help them a bit.

Rose had the misfortune of having a miscarriage but now a new little bundle of joy, Annabelle Marie had arrived in our family. This joyous occasion took place on February 18, 1975, and she was a real little flower to our family.

Manny was fourteen now and didn't want anything to do with a little girl, but she wasn't at home many days until there was a race from the school bus to the house to see who would get to hold her first. She got her share of attention.

She had a cousin born five days after her. Rose made a little swing sort of like a hammock hanging from a log in the living room where Annabelle and Jeremy, her cousin had some good sleeps.

One night one of our neighbor women phoned to tell me she didn't know what to do. Stan had given her son some money to buy some cigarettes and he'd lost the money. I told her, "Oh, don't worry, I'll look after it."

Mark was still with us then and the next evening after chores and supper, there was a nice big package of White Owl cigars brought out. I told the boys they didn't have to sneak around and smoke now that they were men, I had bought them something to smoke. Things went great for a while. They could inhale and blow it out

91

their noses just like men. The party didn't last long and their suppers didn't stay down long, but I didn't need to buy any more cigars.

Our family devotion time was always a great time when we sat around the table and read from God's word. Sometimes in teenagers' minds a lot of people are doing things wrong. With teens a very interesting and meaningful thing to do is when you can have a "tell me my faults night" and everyone can feel free to go around in a circle and tell everyone else what they are doing wrong. It's amazing what can be learned. But it's good and everyone can have some new goals.

Rose and I were getting a lot of opportunities to sing at weddings, receptions, anniversaries, funerals and sometimes in church. We always thought it would be neat to make a singing tape for our family and friends.

For many years I had been elected to teach a Young Peoples' class at the Baptist Church in Worsley.

It is kind of neat to be a part of helping build a Church and then being involved in it. What a different world it would be today if there had never been any Churches built or any Bibles printed. Our generation needs to do what we can for the Lord.

I always had a great love for young people. They have so much life and are always eager to learn. On many occasions we would have them at our place for a fun time and sometimes a camp out.

One night Rose and I were sitting in front of our fireplace, talking about these young people and we decided it would be great to have a whole week of camping away from the phone or anything else and we knew the perfect place! I had built a road through our grazing lease down to the Peace River and also built a cabin there. This was a great place for a youth camp.

With some help from friends we built a pole frame that we could put a tarp over for the kitchen and Worship area. Everyone slept in tents. There were a lot of willing adults to do what was needed. Rose was the cook and had some good helpers.

The first year there were about thirty kids. With a part of the day for Bible study, singing, volley ball, swimming and hill climbing. The week went fast!

One afternoon Blue brought a bunch of horses down for horse back riders. Friday evening was family night so if the weather permitted, Moms, Dads, little brothers and sisters could come, have supper, stay for the evening service and return home. This became an annual event for many years. Time invested in young peoples' lives has some great rewards.

Snow in winter makes for lots of fun for young people with snow machines. A lot of times on Sunday afternoons there would be ten snow machines in our yard. There were always contests to see who could climb the steepest hill.

Sometimes with fun comes accidents.

One night one of the neighbor boys had rolled his Dad's truck and needed my help to get it back on its wheels and going. He knew it would be bad enough in the morning to break the news. So I got up, got dressed and got it back on its wheels and away he went.

One morning, after Manny had been out the night before, the pickup was backed up to the house. I found this very unusual. There was a reason. He had laid it over on its side and it had slid for a way down the road. No one was hurt.

Sometimes it's hard to keep from being upset at some of the foolish things our children do, but we have to allow them to learn from their mistakes so they can become confident people. Without self confidence a person can't accomplish much in life and it takes a lot of doings, from small to great things, to gain what is needed.

In the spring of 1977 the time had come to drive a brand new tractor to the farm. What a treat! It even had a cab on it and a heater in it. The doors were tight with no rattles. What a difference to go from a thirty five H.P.. to a tractor with one hundred and fifty H.P.. This one was a 1370 Case. The first one was a DC4 Case. To be able to have a tractor like this was a real joy. It seemed to make all the hard work worthwhile.

After the crop was put in, we decided to erect a building for storing grain. So using laminated two by fours this building was forty eight feet long, twelve feet wide, twelve foot walls, with four twelve by twelve footbins.

The next summer we constructed another building the same as that, twenty feet away from the first one. Then we put a roof over the whole thing making a good place to park Combines and other equipment or for grain storage if needed. With several neighbor boys and girls helping we pounded six hundred pounds of four inch nails into this building. It was sure great to drive the last nail!

One of my friends had a sixteen year old son that he thought needed to spend the summer on the farm with us. Things went very well until one day this young man needed to drive the pickup over to the field to get something. I didn't check to make sure he had his drivers' license. I just took his word. On his way back on the gravel road, he started to skid. He jammed on the brakes and the truck rolled over three times. It stopped on its side with his head between the top of the door and the ground. There was a dip in the ground that his head just fit into. He had a cut over his ear so Rose took him to the hospital to get checked out. She came home laughing about the phone call he'd made to his Mom and how he had explained that it really was not his fault. No drivers' license, no insurance money and the truck in the bone yard.

We have been very fortunate that we never had a serious accident with all the different young people that worked for us, although there were a few close calls.

One time our youngest son, Stan was grinding grain for the cattle. His pants got caught in the power take off. He grabbed the seat of the tractor and hung on while his pants were being ripped off!

Another time Stan decided to tie a rope to Dave's bike for what reason, we don't know. Dave took off not knowing Stan had tied the rope to his motor bike and after about a three hundred yard drag, the rope broke and Stan was free with just a few scratches.

Manny was out of school now. He had quit school because he said it was boring and had no challenge. He was good help on the farm and was capable of taking a crew to the bush and doing a slashing job.

Sometimes Dads don't know the right directions to persuade their children to take. Things keep changing. We look back and see we should have done differently sometimes. I was taught and tried to teach our children, that one of the most important things in life is to let the Lord be the director and guide of your life.

After a busy winter, spring had come again. In 1979, crops were in the ground and coming good. We now had eleven quarters (one hundred and sixty acres per quarter) of land and most of the trees were cleared off and in cultivation.

We decided it was time for a new Combine so we traded in our two old ones and bought a 1500 New Holland. This combine did a wonderful job of thrashing.

I guess I had big dreams and goals in life. To be able to see a lot of them come true was very rewarding. Through all the different events we were able to keep Sunday as a special day for worship.

Rose, Manny and I all got our Alberta Guides Licenses at the same time. We always enjoyed camping and spending time in the wilderness area. We decided to guide some hunters from Wisconsin and had a great time with them. They went home happy with lots of moose meat. We got to be very good friends with Albert, whose nickname was Frog, Cavanaugh and his family.

That winter we decided to take our family and spend Christmas with my Mother's Mother who lived in Texas. She was my only living Grandparent and we had a wonderful time with her. We had no idea it was to be her last Christmas. It was also good to show our children the old area of my roots.

Our new friends, Frog and Sherry from Wisconsin urged us to come see them on our way home. We had a great time with them. We had no idea they were having marital problems. They split up in the spring.

When Frog called the next spring, to book another hunt, he said he would like to spend some time with Rose and I alone to discuss what was happening in his family. When he came that fall to hunt, he brought three of his friends with him who became our friends as well.

Jinx was one of the men who became a very special friend. Later, we were privileged to get to know his wife, Mary and their three sons. They came several times to hunt wth us and once even came to help us at our ranch in Pink Mountain. Gary, who also came on the very first hunt with Frog, has remained a special friend down through the years.

It was a very successful hunt and they all went home with meat but my heart was troubled as there had been no time for us to have a private talk with just Frog. We had several phone conversations and letters from Sherry, his wife, who was crying out for help.

After we had our crop off and the field work done, I told Rose, "Our children can look after things at home for a few days. I have to go to Wisconsin to spend some time with our friends to see if there is anything we can do. I'd like for you to go with me." We bought our plane tickets and the next evening we were there.

Not knowing where to start, we asked them if we could all four meet together and we did, with the plan to go to the original problem and start from there. It was a wonderful experience.

Most situations can be solved if people will be honest and share their heart. They must be willing to ask for forgiveness and be willing to forgive. They must be willing to bury the past and leave it buried.

His wife had already committed her life to the Lord and while we were there, Frog gave his heart and life to the Lord also. They got back together and were able to raise their three boys together. That created a special bond between us.

One time when three of us were living in a tent working with chain saws in the middle of the winter the snow was deep and it was cold. Both of the young men that were with me gave their hearts to Christ and asked Him to change them and make them into something good. They had both had drug problems. Kerry went back home and took a welding course. He was killed shortly after in a car wreck. After his death, his Mom and Dad drove almost a thousand miles to come and see Rose and I to find out what had changed their son so much. The other young man went to Bible School. I always was glad I had a part in these two young men's lives.

According to all reports the cow numbers were down in Canada. So we decided to keep our heifers over, buy a few more and get some good bulls. We put them in the community pasture at Hudson's Hope. The grass was good and they did well that summer.

When it came time to bring them home, the truck we had hired got to Fort St. John and found that the hill had slid on the Beaton River crossing and closed the road off. So the trucker took the cattle to his place and unloaded them for the night. In the morning he was planning to reload them and bring them around the long way home. But in the morning there was not one heifer left in the corral. Something had spooked them in the night. They had hit the side of the corral and over it went. They were gone!

It was harvest time and every field had swaths in them now, so you can guess what the early morning phone call was about. He said, "Your cattle are scattered all over the country." He didn't have a horse and had to get going to haul more cattle but he did let me know what happened.

We were in the middle of harvest and this meant a great change of plans with no options. Rose, her sister, Shirley and I loaded our horses in the trailer and headed west. In the next few days there were going to be many hours in the saddle. These cattle hadn't been in civilization all summer and they were spooky.

On the second night of the roundup after a long, hard day, we ended up back by a road about ten miles from our truck. It was dark and we were cold and hungry. We decided it best to wait there awhile and maybe I could stop someone on the road and catch a ride back to our truck and trailer, so we wouldn't have to put another ten miles on our tired horses.

I built a little fire in the ditch to warm our hands by while we were waiting. There was a bunch of cows in the pasture nearby. They saw the fire and came over to check it out.

Then a pickup came by, slammed on his brakes and a man jumped out yelling, "What's going on here?" It was his cattle inside the fence looking at the fire. I guess it looked kind of bad all right with cattle all in a corner by a gate in the dark and three people with horses. It took some fast talking and explainig to calm him down. He gave me a ride to my truck and trailer so I could go back and get the girls and the horses. He became a good friend and a great help.

At the end of the third day we had one hundred and fourteen head gathered up. There were six still missing. A month later one of the ranchers called and said there were five head at his place. They had come in with his cattle. We were sure glad to get them.

One was still missing and we supposed it was gone for good. But in April the following spring, I got another phone call and the man asked what my brand was. I told him it was J over Lazy H on the left shoulder. He said, "Man, I've been trying to locate the owner of this heifer all winter. You come and pay the feed bill and you can take her home."

A lot of the old pioneers have passed on but it was good to see the old pioneer ways had not all gone. Some people's ways you appreciate more as time goes on and some less.

The gentle snow flakes had begun to fall again and the ground was white. It was November 1. The ground was frozen and we knew we wouldn't see it again until April. Summers' work was finished and the things that didn't get finished would have to go on next year's list. In the Peace River country there is such a short time to get things done and you don't have many second chances.

Manny was going to look after the logging this winter so he was getting the skidder ready. I had sold two skidders to different boys that worked for me, on terms they could handle.

I had lots of work lined up for winter, enough to keep four different slashing crews busy. The first was to be a tough one. It was in rough terrain. A native man, Peter had been a foreman for me for a few years now. He thought this job would be just right for him and his sons. It was too rough a country to take a big camp into, so I went with them to get them started.

The first morning I woke up with my hair frozen to the wall of the camper I was in. It was pretty cold! We hardly ever had a thermometer with us. Probably if we would have had one a lot of trees would never have gotten cut.

I have been amazed at how warm you can be working with a chain saw in minus thirty degree weather, wearing a pair of green cotton gloves. When you stop to fill with gas and oil and you pull off your gloves that have hard snow crusts on them and your hands have steam rolling off them, you don't stand around and talk very long.

Peter told me he was finished the job and it was ready for an inspection from the Forestry. So I contacted a Ranger and asked for an inspection. There had to be an inspection done and everything OK before I could get any money for the job.

The next day a very upset Ranger called me and said they had taken a helicopter to do the inspection. They had discovered that the cross ditches on the slopes that were supposed to be made from dirt to prevent the water from running down the hill and cutting big ditches in the line, were in fact made from snow.

He said that he would not go back again to inspect unless I had been there myself and made sure everything was done right and that I had to pay the helicopter bill as well. Again, I had no option. I had invested too much by this time to retreat. The ground was frozen hard and the snow was getting deep. This meant snow mobile, tent and a heavy axe to chop the ditches in the frozen dirt across the line at an angle on every hill.

My brother in law Ken, agreed to go help me to do the job. We knew it was not going to be a picnic. The snow was so deep in the mountains and some hills so steep the snow mobiles couldn't climb. One night we had to tie one of the machines to a tree until morning to hold it. Ken had gone down the hill and decided maybe it was too steep to climb back up. I waited to see if he could climb back up the hill. He waved at me to stop. He couldn't make it back up.

The next morning we ditched that hill and seeded it. We thought there must be a way out the other end. So we untied his machine and away he went! We met a few more miles farther. With very sore wrists we hammered away. A week later we were finished and this time it passed all inspection. We were sure glad to have it finished and be home.

The phone rang the next morning. Another foreman told me that he had forgotten to tell me that the creek crossings that had been filled with snow for the Seismic equipment to cross, all had to be dug out. Part of the job needed the brush and trees rolled back out on the line on the hills to stop erosion. It was already coming breakup there and they already had some mud. I needed to bring the Cat right away.

So I loaded the 350 JD Cat on my truck and headed north. With some difficulties getting through the mud to camp, the Cat was soon unloaded on a pile of brush. The foreman gave me a map and tried to give me instructions on the job lay out.

Cleaning the first creek crossing that the Seismic crew had used to get to the other side of the creek didn't take long. There was about

98

six feet of packed snow in it on top of the ice.

At one time these creek crossings were filled full of dirt and logs and left like that. In the spring all of this dirt and logs were washed down the creek. But using snow instead of dirt solved that problem. It was much easier to fill them with snow than it was in some cases to clean them out. After being left overnight, the snow would set and become solid enough to drive over.

Several miles from camp at 2:30 a.m. I was rolling trees back on the line on a steep hill. A stick ripped off a water hose that was connected to a circulating water heater. Before I could get it stopped, I had lost lots of water. I cut the hose and reconnected it. But now, where was I to get any water?

I remembered I had an almost full thermos of hot coffee. So I stuffed in all the snow I could get into the top of the radiator, then poured in hot coffee to melt the snow and refilled it with snow again. By the time my coffee was gone, I had enough liquid in the radiator to go on. You are never beaten until you give up. By the time we were all finished and back home it was time to be finished with bush work.

But an old friend called and asked if there was any way possible for me to go do a job for him. He said, "We flew the job yesterday and creeks are still frozen over in the mountains." How could I refuse an old friend?

With a 4x4 pickup hooked to the front of another pickup pulling a trailer with a bombardier on it and one pushing up the hills, we went as far as we could go. We loaded everything on the bombardier that the five of us would need for a week. The ice crossings were gone out when we got there. Again no option but to plow off into the open water.

We climbed out on the other side of the creek, all O.K. After another mile we came to a very steep hill that we had to go down. With the sun shining on the slope there was about an inch of mud on top of the frozen ground. I knew it was going to be an exciting ride down the hill, especially with a big tree at the bottom.

After sizing up the situation, I knew that we had to let the bombardier down backwards with the winch that was mounted on the front of it.

After we had hooked the cable to a tree, I told the boys, "Boys, if I don't make it, just bury me here on the hill." I knew it would be a big job getting anyone out of here. What a guy won't do for a friend!

I started down backwards and after I broke over the crest on that slick mud I was instantly gone! When the cable tightened, it snapped!

I had time for one backward glance so I could pull the lever to miss the big tree. My heart had a pretty fast beat and I said, "Thank you again, Lord, you did a good job!"

After we were finished back in there, I knew we had to get back up that hill and across the open river and I was in a big sweat until we pulled up and over the top of it with the winch.

After we were finished and back home, I told Rose, "I'm getting weary of all these tough jobs and narrow escapes. I think it's getting close to time for a change." But I had one more job to do. This one was to be the last for a while.

After the crops were in and the cattle out to grass, we built racks on the Cat and bombardier to carry our gear, as we planned to spend the night where ever darkness overtook us.

We loaded up and headed to the mountains again. Every day we were seeing lots of big grizzly tracks. At night there were some big debates about the safety of tent from a bear. Some of the boys chose to sleep out under the stars so they would know which way to run when the bear came.

It was a great crew, the work was hard, the sun was hot and the job was very eventful. One day, Bruce, my brother in law, was driving the bombardier climbing a steep hill. But while it was climbing, it didn't like to turn very good. All of a sudden it started rolling backwards. I didn't know that a tree was about to come into the windshield. He had pushed the clutch so that it would roll backwards, it turned better that way.

Well, I stopped him with the bottom of my dozer, in the center of the radiator that was on the back of the bombardier. I not only stopped him but pushed the whole motor backwards and broke the ears off both sides of the bell housing, bent the radiator in, and the fan took a rip all the way around.

When Bruce crawled out of the bombardier, he said, "What have we done now, Poss?" Poss has been my nickname since childhood. We were fifteen miles from our trucks.

Well, we told the boys to keep cutting and Bruce and I would see what we could do. We took the radiator off and stripped away a lot of the radiator because the cores were broken.

With a skinny nosed little vise grip we twisted over and crimped off all the cores that were broken. We put it back on and put a chain on each side from the bell housing to the back of the bombardier and with a long stick for a twister, we pulled everything back into place. Then we tied the sticks down. We refilled the radiator with water and added a half cup of black pepper. We were back in business again and the radiator had no leaks at all!

We completed the slashing, ditching and seeding lines and returned to the trucks. We still had three miles of total disposal left to do. These are lines that crossed the road and all the trees that had been pushed over by the Cats had to be burned or buried a quarter of a mile back on each side of the road.

Darla and one of her buddies, Rhonda had come along to cook for this job and what an adventure for teenage girls! I'm sure none of that crew will ever forget our camp. We had a big tent sitting on the truck that we had hauled the Cat to the job with. Our kitchen was the goose necked trailer that we had hauled the bombardier on.

One morning in the pouring rain, Bruce was cooking hotcakes. A vehicle went by and Bruce gave a big friendly wave with his hotcake flipper.

With a raincoat on and rain pouring off his cowboy hat he was quite a sight! The passenger in the vehicle took a look, went fifty feet down the road and jerked his head around for a second look. He thought his eyes must have been playing tricks on him but it was a real picture. We had learned over the years not to complain about the cooking, for if we did the next meal was ours to cook. What good, soggy hotcakes those were!

We had three miles of brush ahead of us to bury to complete these disposals. The boys went ahead of me with the chain saws and cut into six foot pieces, all trees that the line cutting Cats had pushed over. Some of the boys were throwing them out into the center of the line. I dug one hole after the other to bury all the brush.

One Saturday afternoon, with only three hundred yards left to go, things just wouldn't work right for me any more. I'd pull a lever to go right and I'd go left, I'd pull the stick to lift the dozer and it would go down. This had been a very high pressure job. Finally, I shut the Cat off, crawled off and said, "Boys, we're going home," and that's just what we did. On Monday we returned and three hours later we were finished and had the equipment loaded and headed for home.

I called the inspector and told him it was ready for inspection. He said, "I'm sorry, but our budget is dry for any helicopter time. Can we get around out there to check it?" I told him, "I don't think so, there's swamp, water and mud in the bottom of every valley."

He agreed to go check it if I would pay the helicopter bill. We landed three times to see if the grass we'd seeded was beginning to grow yet and everything looked good. When we landed back in town he said, "I'll write up an approval right away." I decided it was time for me and Rose to take a little holiday time.

Chapter Seventeen
Our Family Is Growing Up

When a food producer has good weather to do the harvesting in, it is an added blessing. I bought a grain dryer to help with the harvesting and what an invention! Unless it's raining, once you start combining you can put in all the hours you can stand.

One day I filled the dryer with canola and had just got it going when I was called to lend a neighbor a hand. From his place, I looked over to our place and could see a big smoke. By the time I got there, flames were shooting thirty feet high. Canola is full of oil and when it gets hot, it really burns.

The dryer had a big fan and a big flame. The fan blew hot air through the grain to take out excess moisture to a level it would keep in storage and not get hot and spoil. When I got the fan and flames stopped, the fire went out. What had happened was, the canola had stopped circulating in one spot and it got hot and caught fire. We got it cooled down and the canola was all right.

The dryer was damaged quite a bit but repairable. It sure could have been worse. Our granaries were all full, plus a big pile between the big granaries. We had quite a thanksgiving that year.

With an opportunity for a big job, I thought I could do one more winter in the bush at Rainbow Lake and north.

I hadn't forgotten how ten years ago at Christmas I had borrowed twenty thousand dollars, which was my limit at that time. The Bank Manager had faith in me and overdrew my account another twenty thousand dollars for me to pay my men. By the end of April I was back in the blue again at the Royal Bank.

That winter there was a young man on the crew that was to become a member of our family. His name was Ken. Darla was cooking that winter for us, we had really gotten uptown! Up until now we had no cook in the winter camps. What a treat to get to camp and have a hot meal ready to eat when the day's work was finished. Sometimes we even had pies and cakes.

One day Manny told us he had chosen his mate for life.

On March 14, 1981, Manny exchanged his marriage vows with Frances Wasylciw. His Grandad Hale performed the beautiful ceremony in front of many witnesses. What a wonderful choice Manny made for a life long companion.

After a short honeymoon, they came to our camp to help finish with the bush work. The mud was getting deep already. It was good to be finished; it had been a good winter.

Rose and her sister, Shirley with the help of Lisa and Stan had done a good job with the cattle that winter. Stan had become a very capable young man now and was good with cattle and horses. Rose was happy that he was now big enough to be part of her crew. Calving was just about over.

In late March, Rose had decided to take some lessons in skiing. She had a run away on cross country skis down a steep hill. Before she made it to the bottom of the hill, she crashed and broke one of her ankles. She was in a cast and on crutches for six weeks. My good helper was sure slowed down now. This gave seven year old Annabelle and I a chance to cater to her every whim.

We tried to teach our children that there were rewards to be had for working. It might be a horse, bike or snowmobile, sometimes maybe even a few acres of their own crop, so they could see the benefit of working. Our children thought they had to work too much sometimes, but I found out a long time ago, that learning good work ethics was a real asset.

Manny and Stan both enjoyed dirt bikes. They got quite a kick out of seeing how far they could go on the back wheel. But one at a time they both had a bad accident and made themselves a story for life. Again I thanked the Lord for sparing their lives.

Our foster boy, Mark Spackman came to the house one day, walking very stiff with no shirt on. I asked him, What happened, Mark?" He said, "I had my bike going a good speed and decided to try standing up on the seat. The front wheel hit a rut in the road and I went sliding on my back in the gravel". I picked gravel out of his back for an hour then I suggested he best find something different for a thrill the next time. He was one sore fourteen year old for a while.

On a business trip to Calgary, in early March I run onto a used Goldwing Honda Motorcycle that was for sale. It appealed to me so I decided to take it home with me.

My youngest brother, Dick had met this wonderful girl that turned his head causing him loss of sleep. So there was a June wedding in Saskatoon, Sakatchewan for Dick and Shirlee.

Rose and I decided The Goldwing needed some exercise so we rode it to the wedding. What a beautiful wedding and wonderful day in Dick and Shirlee's life.

Shortly after returning home from the wedding, it was time for Lisa's high school graduation. It was another beautiful day and a real milestone for Lisa of which we were proud to be a part of.

On the first of July, 1982, I became aware that even though I had committed my life to the Lord, I had not asked Him to have total control over my entire operation and everything I was involved in. I had become well aware of the fact that if the Lord doesn't bless your efforts, you work in vain. So the best I knew how, I committed everything I had to the Lord and asked Him to lead and guide me and my family.

Sometime in early spring, Darla had informed us that she had chosen her mate for life. They planned their wedding and on July 15, 1982, Darla Hale became Mrs. Ken Ponath. What a beautiful wedding as they were joined as one by Darla's Grandad Hale. Our family was growing. Ken not only became a son in law but a very good friend. For the next seven years we worked very close together and never had a disagreement.

At that time it looked as though Rose and I were going to be left with a big farming operation, so we decided to list our place for sale. Land had been selling good and we had no debt on our place.

We went to the Pink Mountain area in B.C. that year and bought a small undeveloped place that the two of us could live on, raise some cows and have a lot less pressure. At the time we weren't aware that land prices had started to fall and buyers were few.

That winter we pulled out some trees for next summer's building projects. As soon as school was out we were there peeling logs. We cleared and broke four hundred acres of new land. We built a log barn, a log garage and log corrals for cattle. The soil on this new place was very rich and would surely grow lots of hay.

One day Lisa informed us she had chosen a wonderful young man she wanted to spend the rest of her life with. So on July 15, 1983, Lisa Hale became Mrs. Melvin Lubeck when they exchanged their marriage vows. Again, Grandad Hale officiated for this beautiful wedding.

After having two nervous young men ask if I would give them each one of my daughters in marriage and being very happy to do so, I'm very thankful for our daughter's mates. The only thing I asked of my sons in law was that they love our daughters and that they would help teach their children to love and appreciate what the Lord had done for them.

I had been a volunteer probation officer for several years now. On one of the visits to Mark, I was questioned if I would bring five young men that were on probation for a tour of the jail. I agreed to if it was not just going to be a trip to show what a nice facility they had and how good the food was. I was assured that would not be the case.

When we arrived at the Peace River Correctional Institute, I suggested to the tour guide that it probably would be good for me to go on that tour as well. After all, it would be good for me to be able to tell young people what it was all about in there. I was very impressed at what these young men's eyes saw and their ears heard and to see the place where they were to have their noon meal. It was a small room in the bottom of the jail. They called it "the hole." Only one of them ate anything.

While talking with the guide after the tour, I asked him if he thought any of these young men would ever be an inmate. He turned the question to me. I said, "Probably the one in the black jacket." Then he said, "Yes, he'll be back."

Attitudes in life and about life are so important toward our fellow man and toward ourselves, as it is so important to see ourselves as not better or worse than, but as a special person created in the image of God.

I wish every parent and teenager could have seen what I saw that day. To see people live day after day with no meaning and no thought of accomplishing or producing anything, I just had to stop and count my blessings. What a blessing to have parents that had tried to teach me true values in life and had given me a vision.

Chapter Eighteen
More Cattle - More Work

To have a week of family camp, at our ranch in Pink Mountain, B.C., was a special time. Several families from the Church were a part of this, plus some other guests were there. With no appointments or phones to contend with, a good time of fellowship was enjoyed together.

The day we got a phone call at home, that our sister in law, Brenda, had been in a car wreck on her way to a school reunion in Texas was a very heavy one. Not only she, but most of her family was in the hospital. She had a broken back and a severed spinal cord and the doctors said she might never walk again.

Good health and life itself is so often taken for granted. Brenda was a very healthy and helpful mate to Jody. When all you have to work with are your hands, a good mate cannot be valued in dollars.

One night one of our neighbor boys had an accident and was thrown from his pickup. The doctors did what they could for him, but his time was up. To witness death like that, gave life more meaning for me.

Our foster boy, Mark, had come to live with us at thirteen years of age. We learned to love and appreciate Mark. He had a big heart and would do almost anything for us. He had not been "raised", he had just grown up. Every time he would go home to spend some time with his Dad, we had to start all over with him. I spent more time with the school principals because of him than I did for our own five children.

We had two dogs that helped me understand Mark. One was a Border Collie. It was impossible to get that dog to follow a bear's trail, but with cattle he was a wonderful helper. The other dog was a Blue Tick Hound, and had no interest in cattle but was great in following a bear's trail. My hope for Mark was that we could help change some of his interests in a positive way.

Mark developed some good work ethics and after five years went on to work elsewhere. He soon met a girl, Laurie and they got married. One of Laurie's brothers and Mark were not good for each other which caused Mark to spend a year in jail.

After his term in the Peace River Correctional Institute, Mark came back and began living in a little house beside us. Laurie had went on to greener pastures.

Our children put on a twenty fifth wedding anniversary party for us after the fall work was done. It was quite a party! My bride hadn't changed much, just gotten a little prettier. Our family and friends gathered together some money for us to take a trip to Texas which was real nice of them.

We had to postpone our trip from October to April and now it was time to go. Mark was planning to look after things at home for us. Annabelle was going with us, our plane tickets were bought and we were ready.

The day we were to leave, Mark packed all his gear in his truck and told us he was leaving and wouldn't be taking care of our place for us. That kind of put us in a spot. Our daughters, Darla and Lisa, and their husbands, Ken and Melvin, came to our rescue and volunteered to look after things for us while we were gone. We flew to Wisconsin and visited Frog and Sherry and Jinx and Mary. We had a good time in Texas, too with old school mates and relatives. We had a wonderful time and things were in good order when we got home except for one thing. Our darling, Darla had got kicked in the mouth by a new born calf and had a busted tooth.

The government was in the process of building a community pasture for the cattlemen of the area. This meant trees had to be cleared, land had to be broke and cleaned up, grass seeded, fences built, water holes and corrals had to be built.

After some time, some of the pastures were finally ready for grazing. We and a few of our neighbors put cattle in together. We took turns going to the pasture with horses to check the cattle, put out salt, and doctor any sick ones. The next year a manager was hired to do this. We lost a few head that year due to a wild weed called water hemlock.

The following year we formed the Bear Canyon Grazing Association. I had the privilege of serving as president of this Association for the first five years.

What a wonderful bunch of people to work with, for they truly had a pioneer spirit. This mixture of yearling and cow calf owners was new to all of us. It really brought us close together. The real busy days were on entry day in the spring and also when it was time to take them out in the fall. It was a big job but with twenty riders working together, it seemed more like an old time picnic.

As the number of yearlings grew, so did our needs. The association held a meeting and we decided that if we could get a weigh scale on the grounds, and if most of the members would participate, we could have a yearling cattle sale on site and the auction services could be tendered.

With a new goal in mind and a lot of good support, we were able to put it all together and it was a success. The buyers were happy, being able to buy by the truck load and cattle right off the grass was also a plus for them.

To have approximately two thousand head of cattle presorted, have every owner able to feed and water his own and have them ready to sell in about three hours, takes a lot of cooperation. We had a very good manager and good government people to work with. This sale was a first and because it was successful, it became an annual event.

A neighbor at Pink Mountain wondered if we would be interested in leasing his ranch as it joined ours. After a family meeting, Manny and Fran decided they would move up there and look after cattle. We now had eight hundred acres growing hay and with the addition of this new place, the operation would handle at least three hundred mother cows. The plan was to bring the calves back home and finish them out, having them ready to butcher when we sold them.

To start with, we bought fifty bred heifers to go to Pink Mountain. With land not selling, it seemed the only thing to do was raise beef to meet the challenge as cattle prices were pretty good.

Each year we bought more yearlings, some to keep over winter, put on grass the next summer and sell in the fall. We would finish some through the winter and sell them in the spring. With two hundred mother cows and feeding as many calves through the winter as we could put up feed for, we didn't have much idle time.

We had burned two hundred and fifty acres of canola that spring. This was because the rains had come too late for the crop to mature before the frost came in the fall. It was ruined. This all added up to lots of expense and no income.

Two years of bad crop conditions for us and all cost of production increasing, we felt that the only option was to mortgage our land and term out our payments. What a hard day for us as we had said we would never do that. "What is God saying to us?"

After the crops were seeded, I knew we were going to need some extra money. My brother Blue owned a big backhoe. My son in law, Mel and I bought a Cat and we hoped to do some construction work together.

Several contract jobs for Ducks Unlimited were coming up, for the construction of control dams. These were to be built in marsh land areas to maintain the water level for the preservation of wildlife. We bid on some of these jobs and got them. We spent several days building these dams. It proved to be very interesting work.

Due to a long stretch of dry weather, the government initiated a program for the construction of dugouts, to hold water for livestock and residential use. Water wells are almost impossible to get throughout most of the area.

A big hole dug in the clay dirt holds water very well and as there is normally lots of water running in the spring as the winter snow melts, the dugouts refill again. With the government picking up most of the tab and people paying a small portion of the cost, we built lots of water holes.

In the fall of 1986, the winter feed was all up and the harvest was completed. We now had seven hundred head of calves at home, most of which we bought. This left us with a big mortgage payment facing us.

Blue, his son Kurt and I bid on a job up in the Yukon, clearing bush between Haines Junction and Haines, Alaska. Ken, Darla, and Rose thought they could handle the cattle with the help of two other hired hands. With new calves purchased in the fall, you always have lots of sick ones mostly with pneumonia. Of course, it depends a lot on the care they had prior to their arrival. It takes a lot of observing, to detect them being sick in the early stages and get on with treatment.

So with the camp and crew put together for the Haines contract, we headed north on November 6, and what a project we got into!

We had two Cats working double shift, piling and burning fifteen kilometers of roadway. Some of the regulations were very hard to comply with. We were forced to hire a certain percentage of local help at a preset price and we soon found out that these people only worked when the mood hit them to do so.

A lot of the slopes were so steep that the Cats couldn't work on them. My nephew only had a limited time that he could stay and help. When he left, the crews that were cutting by hand and burning a strip of brush fifteen meters wide, were without a foreman.

109

A broken track frame on the Komatsu caused a lot of problems. Also pieces of the drive sprocket kept breaking off, and roller bolts were breaking every shift. It seemed there was no end to the welding that had to be done just to keep it going. There were several tough days, but one morning there were four bottom rollers broken off. This meant lying on your back, welding on to a broken bolt up in a hole to make the bolt long enough to get a vise grip on it to take it out so a new bolt could be put in. I had twelve more bolts to go, when my son Stan came up and said, "Dad, the D6 fell through the ice and it's bad stuck!" Right that instant, here come the Inspector from Whitehorse to look at the job and he said, "Come with me, let's go take a look at what you've been doing."

Well, I had to crawl in with him and leave most of the crew standing there, one Cat broken down and the other one stuck waiting for the 65 Komatsu to get fixed so it could pull it out, wow!

I was already down hearted as I knew this job was losing us a lot of money every day. We bid this job much too low. I guess I wasn't very nice to the Inspector that day when he began telling me what I had to come back and redo, when I was told before that everything was very good.

Two of my brothers in law, Ken and Keith were helping. Ken's wife, Debbie was our cook and what an asset she was. She always had a good attitude as well as being a great cook.

Rose flew to Whitehorse and I met her there. It seemed like years since I had seen my Rose. She was always just like a fresh breath of spring and it was quite a reunion.

It was getting very close to Christmas and we were almost finished. Throughout my years of working in the bush I have never had even several jobs put together, that was as tough as this one. Ken, Keith, Mel and my son, Stan had done their very best to make it work. On my last shift on the Cat, in the middle of the night, Ken came to spell me off. He said, "I know you're beat, go rest a while." I knew he was beat too, but I will never forget that, even if I live to be a hundred. I made it to the truck seat and crashed. I thanked God for my brothers in law.

I contracted the last little part of this job to a local man that owned a backhoe. I knew he could finish burning the piles as they were all made and all on fire.

On December 23, we loaded our camp and headed for home. We arrived home on Christmas Eve, sad, sick and sorry. The Komatsu needed a sixteen thousand dollar repair job. We took an approximate seventy three thousand dollar loss on the job and seven weeks (equal to at least ten years) off my life. What a job!

With all the children and grandchildren home for Christmas and seeing the joy in their eyes caused me to forget my troubles for a while and join in and celebrate the birth of Christ.

The cattle had been well taken care of and they looked good. It felt good to walk among the cattle again. I thought to myself, "These I understand and enjoy working with."

We analyzed our feed several times and discovered what was deficient. We had learned what minerals and vitamins to add and how much to add to get a balanced ration, so we could grow the healthiest cattle possible.

The Komatsu was repaired and ready to go again by the end of January so it went back to the bush cutting seismic lines with Mel as the operator. If we had not had insurance, we would not have been able to get it repaired. Again I questioned, "Lord, what are you trying to tell me?. This valley I'm in is getting pretty deep".

In March, Manny and Fran wanted to be closer to a hospital as they were expecting a new baby, so Rose and I went to Pink Mountain to look after the cows. It was calving time and we always enjoyed that time of year.

One morning, while I was feeding the cows, I noticed one of them coming from the bush down by the creek. I put some hay in the corral for her and locked her in there until I was finished feeding. I figured she had a new baby down there and would lead me to it when I let her out of the corral. Well, when I finished feeding and checking the other cows, I opened the gate and followed her to her new calf. When I got there and saw what had happened to this little calf, I wished all the wolf lovers and animal rights activists in the world could have been there. It was one of the most horrible sights I've ever seen. There was blood all over the packed snow in a large area. The wolves had started eating the calf from the rear end and the little guy was still alive. I found a big stick and finished him off.

I went and got a horse to drag him out of there. The wolves didn't need any more beef as he was number five they'd gotten. I was putting the horse away when I heard the chopper go over. When they got down there, close to where the calf was, the shooting started and didn't stop until there were three wolves and two coyotes dead. I sure was relieved and we lost no more calves that spring.

We got word that Mel had broken through the ice on a swamp with the Komatsu and just the top of the canopy was sticking out. It took two Cats on top of a big pile of snow to winch it up and out of the swamp and water.

111

His brother in law, Ken went to help him. They put a parachute over it with propane torches going, to thaw it out, so all the oil could be drained and replaced with new oil. It took a couple of days and Mel was back on the job again.

Meanwhile, Rose, our second grandson Dwayne, and myself were having a picnic. Little baby calves were coming pretty fast. We were kept pretty busy keeping the pairs matched. We ear tagged the calves to match their mother. Dwayne was quite a knowledgeable little guy and knew where everything was kept. It was his first year in school.

Manny and Fran came home with a little bundle of joy. Here was Dustin, son number three. Now Dwayne and Chris would have a playmate.

Things were going well at Pink Mountain. The new land that we had cleared and put into cultivation was producing good that summer.

Manny had made twenty five hundred big round bales of hay. In the winter the moose also enjoyed spending some time at the hay stack, especially at night. You could hardly build a fence high enough they couldn't jump.

Casey McKenzie, Jerry and Rose in front of Tatogga Lake Resort, B.C.

Chapter Nineteen
One Day At A Time

Big Dave came to work with us that spring. Several of his children helped too, when there was something they could do. His two oldest boys, Jake and Henry were soon operating the machinery.

When it came time to put up silage, it took a big crew. His oldest daughter, Mary drove the swather, putting many acres into windrows for the silage cutter to pick up, chop and blow into a truck. Then it was hauled and dumped in front of the pile. Here it was pushed onto the pile and packed down. With four hundred loads of silage cut, it made a big pile of feed.

I had bought a set of cattle weigh scales from an Auction Mart a few years prior and it was now time to get them installed so we could check on our weight gains to determine if we were feeding the right rations. My brother in law, Keith and his boys came and installed it for me. Now, we could determine the amount of shrinkage on the cattle as they were moved in or out. That winter we fed just over a thousand yearlings. Our losses were minimal and our gains were good.

Stan told us he'd met the love of his life and wondered what we thought of his choice Joanne Briand. We told him we had already fell in love with her and would be proud to have her as a daughter in law. So on March 12, 1988 Grandad Hale performed another beautiful wedding and we gained another beautiful daughter.

Joanne's parents are of French origin and very fine neighbors. About two years prior to Stan and Joanne's wedding, her Dad Raymond, had a serious tractor accident with both his legs being crushed below the knees.

Later, one of his legs had to amputated. He had insurance that would have taken care of the payment due on their farm, but while he was in the hospital fighting infections, etc., some bad decisions were made. They were forced to get off the farm and it was sold. Some time later, Raymond was able to get part of the insurance money back from the organization that sold his land. They had taken the insurance money and had planned to keep it. But Raymond doesn't give up easy and is digging another well. He truly is a pioneer at heart.

The cattle sales were good at the community pasture in September. I thought, "Why couldn't we have a cattle sale here at home as well?" I felt we needed at least a thousand head to be active enough to get buyers to come. In the fall of 1988 we took on three hundred head to custom feed for a neighbor. Rose and I and some of our children bought cattle through the North Peace Feeder Association.

In my struggle to get my finances in order, I sold Ken and Darla, two hundred mother cows, with the proceeds from that sale going to the bank for loan payments.

Ken and Darla's calves were going to be wintered with ours. They had brought all their feed from the land they had purchased. What a pile of feed and what a nice bunch of yearlings. We were wintering just over fifteen hundred head that winter. That meant lots of checking for sick ones, doctoring them and lots of feed to be put out each day.

When December came that year we were not able to make our mortgage payment. One Banker had told me, "If you can't make your payments in three months they could call your loans." I was very nervous about this so in early January 1989, Rose and I went to see the Bank Manager. The Bank had moved our business from Hines Creek to Fairview which meant we were dealing with a new manager.

After visiting with him and expressing my concerns, instead of saying, "Let's look at this and see what we can work out," he said, "I guess you had better go see your lawyer".

He knew I never had a lawyer as I'd never had a reason to have one except to sign a paper at some time or another. He suggested we could go bankrupt. Well, this was all new and strange to me. Never before, had I dealt with a banker that had no intention of any negotiating in his mind.

The previous bank managers knew everything about us, even how to make coffee in our house. Never, had there been any secrets between us. We always had total trust in them, never questioning their integrity or honesty. I have come to realize what a mistake that can be. I had no idea what I was about to get into with the bank.

These people were professionals and I was a novice. When they decide they want what you've got, there isn't much you can do. They have lots of dollars to play with and lots of time. It is unimportant to them, how long it takes to grind you to the place where you have nothing left, not even an ounce of spirit left to kick back.

A friend told me he had a lawyer in Edmonton and he would accompany me and introduce me to him. He knew I was scared to death about all the horror stories I'd heard about lawyers.

After meeting the man and briefing him on what was happening he said, "Well, I guess it sounds like they want you to make a settlement offer to them if that's what you want to do."

I thought about that for a moment and told him, "Yes, that's what I want to do. My dream for many years has been to build a cattle ranch in the Peace River country and now my dream is starting to sink."

We drew up the best and most reasonable offer we could put together for a total settlement with them. After the bank looked at it, they asked for a sworn declaration of our net worth. I listed everything at present market value. What a super, big mistake, because we ended up with fire sale prices and what a difference!

Our bank manager and his friend, an agrologist came out for a visit to see the cattle one day. While they were there it came lunch time so they had lunch with us. During the course of our conversation, we told them we had a date set to have a cattle auction sale right there as we felt it would bring the best results. Two days later we got a nice letter demanding all our debts be paid in full within thirty days. Wow, what great news!

I thought I had some bad days before, but at the age of forty nine and Rose at forty seven, we were about to learn over the next three years what real pain was like when your dream is torn from your heart.

The cattle sale had a date set, so we let it stand. We planned a machinery sale, but the bank said if we did, they would seize all the proceeds from it even though they only had a mortgage on four pieces of the machinery.

I got a call from a friend in the North Peace Feeder Association one day. He said he had just received an interesting phone call from a lawyer representing the bank. They told him they planned to seize all the cattle at my place because the banker had just miraculously heard on the radio that we were having a cattle auction at our place and they were afraid I would run with the money.

I asked him if he could go to a notary and write that all out, sign it and fax it to my lawyer. I told him I would do the same and I'd state in my affidavit how the manager and agrologist had been at our place a few days earlier, had a meal at our table, I showed them the cattle, told them of our plans for a sale and even told them the date of the sale. There were no secret plans.

So the date for the cattle sale came. The cattle were ready and looking good. Buyers from several places in Alberta were there. But, we didn't know until 10:00 a.m. the day of the sale if we could proceed or not. Apparently, the bank had gone before the Judge three times that morning and he finally told them, "No, you can't seize those cattle." Our lawyer called to inform us and the sale went on. The cattle sold well and the buyers were happy.

To make an "at home" sale work took a lot of doing. My brother in law, Ken traveled a long way to help us and I will always be grateful. We also had the help of some real good friends.

The cattle all had to be presorted and weighed into truck load lots. In about three hours, approximately twelve hundred head were sold. Making sure nothing gets mixed up until every animal has been loaded onto a truck and gone, is quite a bit of pressure. That night I had plenty of reasons to be extremely thankful to the Lord for that day.

The people from the Grande Prairie Auction Mart had been great to work with. Lorne had come and given us his very best to help have everything ready for the sale.

The bank got the money from the cattle they had security on. The cattle that we and the children had borrowed money from the North Peace Feeder Association to feed until they were ready to slaughter and then sell, did real good and we were all able to pay off our debts to them. Fred and all the North Peace Feeder Association people had been great to work with and showed a very caring spirit.

If anyone thinks that because they don't have any payments due, that the bank can't or won't call your loans, they are mistaken. It wasn't long after this that they called my son in law, Ken's loans and he didn't have a payment due for six months. I learned then, that the banks have more power than the government does.

Our MLA went to talk to the bank about Ken's loans being called and he told me, "There is not a thing I can do! They are trying to get at you." That incident cost the bank a few customers. This was in the spring of 1989 and what a learning expedition I was in for. Up until this year I thought the banks were totally honest and trustworthy.

The manager told me all my old records had been destroyed. I had not made a practice of keeping every paper pertaining to bank business. Why did I need to? I trusted them! I know now, that I should have goten a copy of everything I'd signed and kept it on file at home.

After finding that they did have the records and how much it would cost to get them, I was able to acquire my old records. The Borrowers Advocate went through them and concluded that over a period of eight years, according to their finds, we had a wrongful overcharge in interest of over three hundred and forty thousand dollars. By the Borrowers Advocate's standards, one of my friends received a cheque in the spring of 1994 for interest overcharge, but of course he had to agree to keep it quiet.

My lawyer suggested that I lease the land out to someone with cattle so it could be grazed and it would bring in a little revenue to pay some bills, of which we had our share.

The bank had overdrawn my checking account eight thousand dollars in interest, so I sold my 350 JD Cat and gave them the money. They did a super job in tying my hands. The next thing the bank did was sue some of our children for "unjust enrichment." This tied the children's hands and made them feel like criminals.

On one visit to Edmonton, one of the head bank men said, "Anyone knows if you feed a cow a thirty dollar bale of hay that means she's worth thirty dollars more." Wouldn't it be great if it always worked like that?

In the absence of our lawyer, he had left one of his associates in charge of us. It was at this time the bank pushed very hard to get everything their way.

Another dear friend helped me buy another one hundred and twenty days that was badly needed. When you live in an area for thirty five years it's wise not to go burning bridges as you never know when you might have a need. We had a lot of friends who were very supportive.

On one trip to Edmonton to see our lawyer's associate, we were given a huge assignment. They wanted us to match all of our bills with all of our cheques, back to August the year before and now it was June. Then I was told that it looked like the bank was going to get everything we had and everything we were ever going to have. It was now the end of the day and time to drive the four hundred miles back home.

Words cannot describe how I felt, except I knew what the lady meant when she wrote that great poem, "Footprints in the Sand." I was completely blown away. I know what people feel like when all they see is doom and I understand why some commit suicide. I could never have understood this kind of pain without being there.

A real help to me was when I read how one time God sent an Angel to strengthen his Son when He was in great need. So, I thought it's all right if we need to ask for some special strength sometimes. He gives it just when we really need it. I was in tremendous need of God's extra strength now.

After my lawyer returned to office duty, he suggested that I should figure out what I was going to do, as the bank was probably going to get the ranch. This was no easy thing to decide as I had no trade of any kind, no grade twelve diploma and I was almost half a century old. How was I going to provide for my Rose and Annabelle who was now fourteen?

The atmosphere was different now at the ranch we had built and were now going to lose. Mother had come to visit for a while one day and when she went home she told Daddy it was just like a morgue at our place. I guess there was some resemblance all right.

Manny, Fran and their three sons had now moved to Terrace, B.C. to do some charter fishing. So Rose, Annabelle and I went for a visit and to help with whatever we could. While we were in Terrace that summer, Rose had to make a trip back home to get her driver license renewed. Hanging on the front door was a piece of paper, stating that the bank had seized all the cattle there and some oats growing on part of the land. There was a number to contact on the bottom of the paper. I'm sure the bank had a big smile the day the sheriff phoned them and told them it was done.

I phoned the sheriff, who was the contact person and asked what they were doing seizing someone's cattle other than mine and that it would probably make someone very mad to have a hundred and fifty thousand dollars worth of their cattle seized for no reason. She wondered what my brand was. I told her, "The bank knows my brand and you should have known it before you went out there!" There was dead silence on the phone. I'm sure the smile was not there on the second call to the bank.

A week later a friend got a call to inquire if he had seen a seizure paper in the field of the half section he was leasing from me. He told them he had not and they asked him to bring in a copy of our lease agreement. He called me, thinking his work on the place was in vain.

I told him not to worry, nothing had been to court and now they were trying to bluff him.

After he took his lease agreement into the bank manager, the bank's lawyer phoned him and told him not to pay Jerry any more lease money until they gave the O.K. This left both the manager and the lawyer liable for a charge.

Shortly after this, a nephew and his wife were renovating a house they'd bought to rent out. They were using gas to loosen tiles on the basement floor and had carefully turned off all flames and pilots in the house. Barb was sweeping around the furnace and picked up a lighter stick for lighting pilot lights. To see if it still worked, she gave it a flick and there was a big explosion of fire. Before they could get out of the house, Russ had sixty five percent of his body burned and Barb had ninety five percent. They were rushed to Edmonton by air ambulance. She was not expected to live through the first night but she did. Several skin grafts took place and she was finally able to leave the hospital. It is a real miracle they are both alive.

Not long after this accident happened, Rose's Mom, Florence took sick. Cancer was diagnosed and she under went surgery in Edmonton. Three weeks after the operation she went to be with the Lord, October 22, 1989.

Ken's Dad, Jack fought Leukemia for a long time, but it finally took it's toll and we buried Jack a month after Florence.

Another friend that had been with me in Oklahoma when I had my car wreck, had been battling cancer for some time and he lost the battle and we buried Norman shortly after Jack.

In early December, Rose and I decided to have a benefit music night for Russ and Barb to help out with hospital expenses. I thought if I had been capable of continuing leading the song service at church through all these events, even if sometimes I had questioned, "Father, why have you forsaken me?" then we could probably put one together. There were lots of musicians and singers in the area so again with a pioneer spirit and lots of willing help we put on a four hour program, just over twenty seven hundred dollars was raised for Russ and Barb.

We were still on the home place but the soup was getting pretty thin now. I had lots of talks with myself about what I should or shouldn't do as the bank would probably get it anyway. I was used to seeing opportunity, then working on it, but now I had to talk myself out of trying to make it work. I could easily see how a person could get feeling sorry for oneself and just sit down and do nothing. It sure looked like my family and I had done all that work and spent time apart for nothing. But after looking at my roots and with God's help I knew I couldn't do that.

In all of this one of the toughest things was when I heard someone's comment, "Serves him right," or "He had it coming."

I went and talked to a friend who said he'd give me some contract bush work and would make sure I got the money. Once again I started making plans to go to the bush. Ken Rohl was my friend as a young man and has been through the years. He said he would like to come and put the winter in up here working with me. He is now from Calgary. He, his son Keith, his son in law John, and their friend Chris, run one crew. Ken Ponath, my son in law, run another crew and we had a good winter.

When the bank demanded Ken and Darla's loans be paid in full in thirty days, it was amazing what happened. When their cows were put up for sale, most of the buyers knew what was going on and once again "fire sale prices" were offered for these cows. Fortunately a man that wanted some good cows came and bought them and Ken and Darla were able to pay the bank off.

But the Bank still had their hands tied. They had to get another lawyer; that meant more expense for Jerry and Rose, as we felt it our duty to pay all legal fees.

Their cow herd was pretty well picked over by now. There were only a few left; the oldest and the poorest. It was like one well had gone dry and it was time to pick up the shovel and dig another well. 1989 had been a year to ever be remembered. It had been a one day at a time year.

Theses current events were causing me to look at priorities and values in life as never before. I concluded that the real values are the things that can't be taken away by some person or organization.

Chapter Twenty

New Hope

Everything was different this spring after the bush work was over. There were no cattle in the corrals. There was no milk cow for Rose to milk as she'd done for the past thirty years. There were no chickens, nothing but a cattle dog with sad mournful eyes. I had decided that my heart wasn't going to stop even if part of it was being torn out and the sun did still come up every morning.

We saw no reason to plant a garden because next week it might all be over and we'd be gone. After a while I got to where I thought, "Well I've agreed to give them everything they have security on and that's not enough, we just don't have to be in a hurry to do anything."

We planned to have a Just For Fun Music Night at our place this time in June 1990. Again it was mostly local talent and we had a great time.

We were afraid we might have to cancel it as it rained lots, but the weather turned nice a few days before and we held it out in the open air. The planned program lasted until about 11:00 p.m., but the music around the campfire lasted for most of the night. Some people had brought their motorhomes.

The next morning we had a free pancake breakfast. Then a neighbor took off his hat and went around collecting some money for Rose and me. What a special gesture, for it told us he really did care.

One day we picked up our mail and there was a nice card in it, simply signed, a friend. It listed two Bible verses in it. One was in

Matthew chapter six, verse six where it says when we pray to enter into our closet. The other was in Deuteronomy chapter six, verses ten and eleven where God told Moses he would have houses he didn't build and wells he didn't dig. We still to this day do not know who sent it.

I never knew the feeling of someone bringing food to our house just to say, "We care," until Rose's Mom passed away. Friends and neighbors knew there was family coming from far away and that some would be staying with us and what a sobering and touching feeling when they brought food to our house.

I was having a very bad time trying to put together something to do next after the ranch was gone. Rose and I had always worked together wherever possible. Now at the fifty mark, it just didn't seem like a nine to five job was for me! I had tried that for a little while as a machinery salesman. It seemed there must be something we could do together. We thought perhaps in Bella Coola, B.C., but nothing came together there.

I guess one of the biggest problems I had was the feeling that God had taken his blessings from me. That left me totally at a loss, as I couldn't put my finger on why. It doesn't seem to matter how intelligent a person is or how hard they try, if God chooses to with hold his blessings, nothing will happen. I got my license for selling Real Estate but that never came to amount to anything. Perhaps I didn't give it a chance, but my heart just wasn't in it.

When the school term was finished, Rose, Annabelle and I packed up again and headed back to Terrace, B.C. since we didn't have anything at the home ranch to stop us.

We put in a good two months staying with Manny and Fran again. We helped with the charter fishing, mostly on the ocean. We were out where the big salmon live and once in a while we got into a halibut bed. What a picnic that was! Then it came time to go back to Alberta, to get Annabelle back in school.

I was reading the newspaper the night before we departed for home and noticed there was a Resort for sale up the Stewart Cassiar Highway. We decided to go look at it.

What a beautiful part of the world with the majestic mountains, vast lakes, rivers and steams with lots of fish and wildlife. We liked what we saw, but were in no position to do anything just yet, not until we were finished with the bank!

Annabelle and her grade all ended up on correspondence for the school term that year and that was a new challenge for her. What a time in her life for all the roots to be pulled out and all the securities of home to be falling apart. She was such a special flower in our home with such a quiet spirit and easy to get along with. I was sad to think that some of the things we had been able to teach her brothers and sisters about life on the ranch would not be passed on to her. This tore at my heart. I guess all this was why I had some bad thoughts about bankers. Especially the bank that had called my loans and gave me only thirty days to pay and then tried to close all the doors on me with no negotiating.

Since there had been no court yet, it seemed the bank was hoping to get me with fraud, or unjust enrichment, or that I'd just agree to anything.

I had told my lawyer when I first met him that I was a homesteader and that meant something. A person could never give up and be a homesteader, for there are several tough days involved in homesteading.

Rose and I were back to saving nickels and pennies. So far bush work had always been best for us so that was the plan for another winter.

My lawyer and I were getting well acquainted by now and he assured me someday it would be over with the bank and Rose and I could carry on a normal life. I chose to believe him as so far he had called their moves very close. The bank's lawyer was very motivated to settle, for if it went to court they could not handle the bank case against me because they would be on trial for defamation of my character. So, there we sat with time to make some money for whatever was coming.

In the spring of 1991 the friendly bank manager phoned one day to say that the bank had decided to sell our land back to us if we would come up with a fair offer. He invited us to come in and see him. It smelled like a trap so I invited my Dad to come with us as a witness. The manager had a witness with him too.

Well, at the meeting in the bank, the manager assured us if we would come up with a reasonable offer and even told us what that was, that they would in fact sell it back to us. Up until then they always said they couldn't sell it back to us under any terms.

So, we went to the Farm Credit Corporation and they agreed to help us get the money needed to buy it back. I hand delivered the offer and told the manager where we would be getting the money from. Two days later he called me to tell me they really couldn't do that; it was against bank policy. I thought it was a trap and sure enough it was. When they concluded we would have to borrow most of the money, that ended that.

For over thirty years Rose and I had sang at a lot of wedding anniversaries, funerals, church specials and several community functions. Different people had asked us if we ever considered making a tape. We decided now, we had time to make a tape as we had no crop or garden to plant or cows to look after.

We made our first tape with the help of a nephew Harvey and a very good recording artist Lorne, in June 1991. We called this tape "Beyond the Sunset," that is a mixture of gospel and love songs done in country style. It was another first for us and we enjoyed doing it very much.

Ken and I had an opportunity to get a big backhoe and put it to work for the summer. It was a rental purchase deal and we used part of our winter bush work money for the first months rent. That venture turned out good.

Rose and I took another trip up the Stewart Cassiar Highway in April to see how late the deep snow stayed in the spring. When we got up there we found that the next place up the road was possibly going up for sale. The owner had gone trapping in November and failed to come out for Christmas as expected. He was no where to be found. The place was closed down of course, as he usually hired all his staff. This place was under a blanket of snow, not quite as deep as the other place we had come to see.

When we returned home, I called the bank manager and asked him where we were heading, if there was any way of settling this thing. He said, "I'm not supposed to talk to you anymore." I told him, "O.K., I understand that, but you are leaving me no choice but to sue you and your lawyer" and hung up the phone. It seemed to me like it was time to load his brain a bit, mine had been overloaded for some time now.

I called my lawyer and told him what I had done and that we were considering leasing the Tatogga Lake Resort for a while this summer, if it all came together.

We got a phone call saying that the owner, Mike Jones of the Tatogga Lake Resort had been found in May, in Bowser Lake after the ice had melted. He and his snowmobile had gone through thin ice and the place was up for lease.

After arriving in Terrace we were able to get in touch with the Curator for the Estate and got some details about who to get in touch with personally in the area of the Resort.

Jerry and Rose - Tatogga Lake Resort owners

"Grandpa" 93 year old father - in - law Dick Dixon at Tatogga Lake, B.C.

Road right of way clearing at Haines Junction, Y.T.

Chapter Twenty One
Count Your Blessings

On July 1, 1991, Rose and I arrived at the Resort to check it out. The place had been closed since October and now it was July. It looked like a big enough challenge. It is nine miles south of the little village of Iskut and at the end of the phone and power lines.

Marvin came down with the keys, showed us and told us, everything he could about the place. Rose and I both agreed what a wonderful man he was. He became a very good friend to us and we found he had a real love for the Lord. He was always doing special things for us and we and lots of other people in the Iskut Valley learned to appreciate and love him very much.

The property went from the highway to the lake, so Rose and I walked down to the lake. When we got down to the lake it was gorgeous.

Across the lake, beautiful snow capped mountains reached up into a clear blue sky. We stood and looked at the vastness and beauty with our arms around each other and big tears that we couldn't keep back. Now, we knew what the card in the mail with no name on it was all about.

My Rose has been such a support and strength for me in so many ways. Often I would be feeling like it was the end of the road for me and Rose would say, "When the time is right, the Lord will let us know what is next for us." What a blessing she has been for me.

But, one day Rose was down. She was sitting in our then very bare living room and she solemnly declared, "Jerry, if we don't get this mess with the bank cleared up soon, my life is just over." The way she came out with it I just had to bust out laughing. Then we both had a good laugh over the pickle we'd gotten ourselves into.

So often I've wanted to blame someone for anything that goes wrong. Especially if it is a major catastrophe, I am inclined to blame God but in all reality, most of the time it is my own doing that gets me in a mess.

Well, after looking the place over, we went back to Terrace and made an agreement over the phone with the Curator to lease the Tatogga Lake Resort for two months. This consisted of a big log building that served as restaurant with living quarters upstairs. There was a small garage for fixing flat tires and whatever came along. There were five rental cabins close to the restaurant plus four more rustic log cabins down by the lake. Also included were gas and diesel pumps. There was also an R.V.park, three boats, three canoes and a Cessna 180 airplane on floats. We had a tentative agreed upon price to purchase, as it was still tied up in court.

We filled our pickup and camper with groceries and things that would be needed to open the restaurant.

Manny had some time between guiding fishermen clients, so he, Fran and the boys loaded their pickup and the boat he was pulling on a trailer, with oil and things needed to open the gas bar and shop. Then we all headed the six hour journey back to Tatogga. Rose and I both had a renewed lease on life. Maybe there was still something we could do together.

Our first night there was a busy one. By morning twenty three mice had been caught and disposed of. With a lot of long hours every day, we soon had the place ready to receive guests. On July 15, 1991, we put the "OPEN" sign up.

Our daughter in law Fran, was a very good little cook. She could make those eggs come off the grill so over easy. What a sweet heart she always has been to us and now to come and put in all those long hours over a hot stove. Words cannot describe the gratefulness I felt as I watched Fran and her Mother in law working side by side. It wasn't long and the place had a reputation for "Stop at Tatogga they have good food there."

Manny and his family were so much a part of the opening of the place. As always, he had a clear mind and knew just what had to be done next. Dwayne wasn't very big yet, but he liked to help at the gas bar. Some of the tourists got quite a kick out of him. They'd try to fool him with the US exchange, but he was nobody's fool.

Chris liked to help with the window washings, but he wasn't quite tall enough for most rigs. There were plenty of boy jobs for him and Dustin to do, which included hauling trailer loads of garbage from the campground every day.

We were only there a few days when Murray came into the picture. He came down wondering if there was a chance he could bring the airplane down and base out of Tatogga Lake. I told him I wasn't interested in stealing him away from the place he was at. He said,"You can't steal a happy customer". So he moved his base down to Tatogga. That was an added blessing for us.

He was busy flying people back into the different lakes and rivers in the mountains to go canoeing down the beautiful Stikine River, or hunting, or back packing, or sight seeing in one of the Parks.

We were instantly very busy as we were in the middle of a tourist season. Just prior to our coming to Tatogga, Rose had told me she was ready to get to work doing something. Well, here she had something to do, and she was happy doing it. I had always accused her of being a work aholic and one day while we were still in Alberta, my accusations were confirmed.

I was working in the bush that winter and as we were heating with wood and I had access to lots of it, I'd bring a pickup full of wood home sometimes. We'd split those big blocks at home. Well, this particular morning, I got up knowing it was cold out as I could hear the logs snapping and popping as all log houses do when it's cold and checked the thermometer. Then I dived back into our cozy bed. Rose asked how cold it was and when I told her, "It's minus forty two," she sat up and said, "What a marvelous day for splitting wood!"

When I told her I knew now for sure she was a work aholic she said, "No, I'm not, I'm a lazy person. It's just much easier to split when it's forty two below!"

We all had much to learn at Tatogga, as it was another first for us. In a lot of ways this was another pioneer project. Living in the area were a lot of pioneer people nine miles north of us. There had been no road through here until 1972, so these native pioneers had worked very hard for their living, trapping in the winter and some working for outfitters in the fall.

They were good woodsmen. The women had to be good with their hands as well, to provide clothes for their families as much as possible.

It was very hard work to take a fresh moose hide, lace it into a big square frame made of poles and then scrape all the hair off. After that, it had to be all fleshed before the tanning procedure began. All the work that goes into a tanned hide is tremendous. The soaking, stretching and smoking, with just the right kind of wood before it is finally ready to sew into mukluks, mittens, moccasins or whatever. Some of these ladies talked of tanning thirty moose hides in one fall. There were a lot of large families with no modern conveniences then. A good part of the year they lived in tents. In the winter their method of travel was by foot or dog team. Usually once a month a trip was made to Telegraph Creek to trade furs for supplies.

There were lots of hardships for the men as well as the women. Life was like this for most of these people into the nineteen sixties. Now a lot of the beautiful handwork that was done on leather at one time is gone, as the younger generation has no desire to do it.

The pioneer spirit still remains in a lot of ways though. If you are hungry, someone will share with you or if you have a need, someone will help you.

In the spring of 1991 Rose and I had gone to an auction sale of a neighbor that was moving away. When a riding lawn mower came up for bid, Rose said, "Buy it." I said, "For what?" but we bought it and an old school bus.

Now, here at Tatogga, I knew why we had bought the mower, for with a big RV park and a lot of other areas to cut, we needed it.

Our son, Stan and his wife, Joanne came up to help, bringing Annabelle and a nephew Barry. They also brought this newly acquired lawn mower.

After getting the yard cleaned up, grass mowed, gas pump going, water leaks stopped and restaurant operating, Rose and I made a quick trip back to Alberta to do some business. We also picked up our "Beyond the Sunset" tapes that were now ready. We were able to sell quite a few tapes in the gas bar and restaurant as souvenirs.

All of our children spent some time helping us get the place going again. We were kind of sad when the end of August rolled around and everybody headed back out so their children could attend school. When our children were small, there were many happy times. When they grew old enough to start trying their wings, one by one, a piece of our heart was torn out.

As parents, if we allow ourselves to be beat down with guilt it can destroy us. When we do the very best we know how, to bring them up with the teachings of the Lord, then there comes a time, one by one, when we have to say, "Lord, I know I've failed in some areas. I did the best I could, you gave them to us for awhile and now we give them back to you." Now, here were all our children, pitching in to do what they could to help us.

A very interesting man stopped to camp with us one night. He showed me some pictures of Roy Roger's horse Trigger that he had done a life size mount on. He was a very hurting man as after many years together he and his wife had gone their separate ways.

The family of the deceased previous owner Mike, came up for a memorial service in August. It was good to get acquainted with his ex-wife, daughter, brother and one of his good friends. We never had a chance to meet Mike and sometimes wished we could have. He must have been an interesting man.

Our lease time went by quickly and now I couldn't find the Curator to find out for sure about us buying the property. The last time I had talked to him, he said, "No deal." This really bothered me. I asked the Lord if we had misread the signs, as it seemed like this was the place where he wanted us to be. We packed up everything we had brought with us and were ready to leave.

Out of the two months we were there our phone had been dead five weeks and was still dead. I told Rose, "I think I'll go up to a phone and call the Mother in Massachusetts and talk to her." She answered the phone and said, "Yes, we want to sell it to you." We made an agreement over the phone.

I didn't know how I was going to do this, as we still weren't settled with the bank, but I knew that the Lord knew and he also knew what was next. So I went back and told Rose the news and we unpacked and spent another week doing things that badly needed to be done.

Our very dear friends, Frog and Sherry and their son, Aaron had come up to see us. They were a big help as there were still many things to do here before we could return to Alberta to wind up things there. Frog and Sherry had come to spend Christmas with us in Alberta in 1990 and had also come to Terrace to go fishing and be with us in June 1991.

When we got back to Alberta our lawyer called and said, "I've got some good news. The bank is ready to settle with you and I think you should take their offer. They will drop all charges against every one of you if you will pay them ninety thousand dollars cash, sign over seventeen hundred and sixty acres, all the buildings and move off." What a brain full of mixed feelings now. For sure the dream would be gone. A friend told me once, it was as much fun building a boat as it was to sail it and I had truly enjoyed building this dream.

I thought of a couple, whom another friend and I were visiting one day and we got talking about God. Tom said, "Aw, we're just like a cabbage. When we die we just rot and that's it." Pansy said,

"No. I don't think so and I've always wondered how I could become a Christian."

After she had prayed and asked Jesus to come into her heart and make her one of his children, my friend asked her, "Now, what are you going to say when the Ol' devil comes by and says, boy did you make a fool of yourself yesterday?" Tom sitting off in the other room yelled out, "Tell the Ol' devil to go to hell!"

That really was how I felt. The Lord had permitted the devil to give me a real workout but now I could tell him, "Devil, go to hell!" My mind was set and beyond all doubt. "As for me and my house, we would serve the Lord."

I went over my priority list and made several changes. At the top of the list were things that can't be taken away by man. I had been permitted to learn some tremendous lessons even though some were very hard. Just to know that Jesus comes in the midst of a storm to rescue us gives me a real peace.

Rose and I had a meeting in Cochrane, Alberta to attend, as we are on the Advisory Board of the new and only Southern Baptist Seminary in Canada. We had to get right back to Worsley, as we could now have an auction sale of our remaining machinery and household things that we wouldn't need and winter was coming fast!

So on October 28, 1991, four days after our thirty second wedding anniversary we had the sale. It was a cold day with about eight inches of snow. We had a big fire going in the shop, lots of good food and coffee and lots of good company.

The farmers didn't have much money to buy with, but lots came for support. A lot of things I couldn't watch sell as there were just too many memories with it. Rose and her girls took some movie pictures but we still haven't been able to watch these either. Someday we will, but not yet.

A lot of things went very cheap, but we appreciated everyone that bid because we knew things were tight. The house was empty now, but we knew there were beds, tables and chairs waiting for us at Tatogga. That day is etched in my mind much like a funeral. I knew with God's help that me and my family would get it back. This had just been a little test to see if I would give up on God. But not a chance.

About the middle of December 1991, we signed the settlement papers with the bank and the very next day we signed the ones that made us the new owners of the Tatogga Lake Resort. Isn't it amazing how in God's timing, everything fits? Sure enough, Rose and I were free again to live a normal life, even if it meant a brand new chapter for us.

In January, Annabelle, Rose and myself took my Mom and Dad back to the place of my roots and to let my brain cool and catch up with what was going on. I have some wonderful Aunts and Uncles living there yet that have been a real encouragement for me. I know they have talked to the Lord on my behalf many times. To be able to go to worship at the country Church at Elmont, Texas where I went as a boy and asked Jesus into my heart added a special blessing for that day.

On our way home we stopped in Jacksonville, Wyoming and took a sleigh ride among an elk herd of over eight thousand head while they were being fed. What a thrill in itself!

We arrived back at the ranch about February 1, and it was time to start making our move to Tatogga. We had agreed to keep the house warm to prevent any freezing problems and in return we had a place to live until we could get moved. We knew a move in the winter would be tough as there were several mountain passes we had to go through. Now, we knew why we had bought the old bus, as we could haul a lot of things in it.

The Cleardale Community gave us a silver tray one night as a going away present. We had enjoyed making our home there for the past twenty years and had made many friends.

Our children had all went to the school there, where I was the first School Trustee. We had entertained and been entertained in that school many times. Many precious memories flooded my soul that night. As we left the Community with the final load of our belongings our hearts were sad.

Our last Sunday at the Worsley Baptist Church, a pot luck dinner was held in our honor and we were presented with a beautiful handmade quilt with scripture verses and all the ladies from the church's names embroidered on it. Many eye were wet as we bid each other farewell for there were many, many precious memories that we'd hold dear for the rest of our lives. We had been a part of a pioneer Church and to leave this family behind hurt more than words can tell.

Rose was the first convert of this Church when it was still a Mission and now she and I would be moving on to a new life and a new chapter.

Chapter Twenty Two
Starting Over

In some places on our move, there were snow banks on the side of the road as high as the bus. The roads were kept open all winter and were in good shape. After three trips and three weeks we were able to be at a place we could call "Home" again. What a wonderful feeling!

Our home was a big log building with living quarters upstairs above the restaurant. It was heated with mostly wood and took a big wood pile.

We knew for the next few years it would take a lot of work to get the business and appearance the way we wanted, but we knew we were both still very healthy. Now we could think normal even though we knew it would take some time for the scars of the battle we'd just come through to heal.

Our watching our pennies and me going back to work in the winter had paid off. Now we had a home, no mortgage and very little money to have to worry about. Between legal fees and the bank, it had taken about one hundred and fifty thousand dollars plus eleven quarters of land for all the books to be balanced and zeroed. The Lord has given us the ability to accept the things we cannot change.

Annabelle was on correspondence and doing quite well. She was a big help now. Our home got a good wall washing and varnishing right off the bat.

Two neighbor boys had helped us move. Jake returned home but Cornie stayed on to help for a while. We had bought a nice big cook stove and grill and one wall had to be moved to accommodate it.

Ken, Mel and Ken's brother Dave, brought up the last load of things that needed to be moved. One was the trailer that Harvey had built to stay in while working in the bush. Now this trailer would be useful for staff to stay in. When the boys left for home, Cornie went with them. Annabelle, Rose and I stood and watched them drive out and I must admit we felt a little abandoned.

A former owner of the Resort phoned and said he would like to sell the fourteen acres that he had subdivided off, prior to his selling the Resort. He said it was deeded from the highway down to the lake, with a house close to the lake. He said, "If you can make the down payment, I'll carry the rest."

Rose and I decided it would make a great place to live if we ever sold the Resort, would prevent any close competition and if needed, some of our summer help could stay there. We also thought it would be a good place to have a worship time on Sundays. So, we signed the agreement papers and once again we were in debt.

By mid May 1992, we were ready for the summer. With Caravans booked, lots of hunters, canoeists and sightseers booked for the plane, it looked like a busy summer coming up. We had boats and canoes for rent and a lake with lots of rainbow trout. We knew if we had the urge, we could go catch fresh trout for our supper any time.

Keeping all the different inspectors happy was a full time job. There were several things that needed changing. The fire extinguisher inspector said, "You sure need a different hood over the stove. It is far short of what is required." The electrical inspector left a long list. Environment people were making rumbles about all underground gas tanks.

But, what a nice place to meet a lot of wonderful people from all over the world. There was never a complaint from the European people about anything. They were a real pleasure to deal with and they honestly care about keeping our environment clean.

Annabelle decided it was time for her to try her wings on her own and what a hole she left in our hearts. We could see heartaches and tears ahead for her, but we had not stopped the other children and we had to let her go too.

We just trusted that with our teaching and help from the Lord, even though she had to go through some deep water, he would go with her as he had with us and bring her safely out on the other side.

One night I was talking to the Lord about her and He spoke to me so clearly, "She is my little flower too and I am still in control." Then I knew it would be all right. It was very hard for Rose and I to watch our last one leave the nest.

We hired a good staff to work with us, in order to have a place with a good reputation. Our lawyer brought his son Casey to spend the summer helping us. He turned sixteen that summer.

When his parents came to get him in time for school, we had a special going away party for him. Pay day for Casey was in a big sock stuffed full of ones, twos, fives, a money order and a few credit card slips someone had accepted and shouldn't have. Lots of cold hard cash, but he earned every bit of it. It would be great if every situation could end like ours, with your lawyer and his family becoming friends.

Barry, our nephew was always a lot of fun and the Tourists loved him. He was a great help and I've always had a soft spot in my heart for my nieces and nephews anyway, so it was good to spend some time with this nephew. He stayed with us until the end of November.

Shelley was just like one of our own and even called us Mom and Dad. She came at a time when Rose really needed her, therefore, a special bond was always between them. She could take care of the restaurant if Rose wanted to be gone out for a while. She was always happy and good to get along with.

Barry's sister, Jackie also came up to give us a hand for a while that first summer. She was a great help for nailing tin on the roof of the shop as she wasn't afraid of heights. She was also a very efficient waitress and we missed her when she went home.

Rose painted a scripture verse on the wood shed which I thought was always kind of neat. When you came up from the lake, the first thing you saw was "Great is our God and Greatly to be Praised."

We got to help a lot of people in need. Some had no money, but were hungry and were willing to scrub the floor, do dishes or chop wood. Some needed gas or tires, but had run out of money, so I soon learned to keep some projects for people to do who were stuck.

One day a man came in with a broken cross member on his truck and was pulling a big fifth wheel stock trailer. He wondered if I could weld it for him. He had been to Alaska, hauling the world's largest living steer that he had sold. On board his trailer was the largest living horse, with feet the size of a five gallon bucket. Before he left we had a great time, for I found out he had a real appreciation for what God had done in his life.

Another man came back one day and looked me up. He said, "I just wanted to thank you for taking the time and telling me about Jesus, I am now a new Christian and He has turned my life around."

Early in December some people came by, moving from Dallas to North Pole, Alaska. They were in an old pickup that was very heavily loaded and pulling a trailer that was also heavily loaded. They had all their earthly belongings with them. After I sold them some gas, they were ready to go and their pickup wouldn't move. The transmission went out right there. They almost cried, they didn't know what to do. They said they had just enough money to buy gas to get them where they were going.

Rose and I discussed what we could do and decided we could put them up until we could have a transmission brought in by the freight truck, which came twice a week. We would have to pay for the transmission, put it in for them and maybe someday they could pay us. It was already winter and cold, so that's what we did. Meanwhile, they helped us on a bear rug we were finishing and anything else they could do. We took them ice fishing and had a great time with Fred, Dorothy and her handicapped sister. Fred was quite handicapped too.

Sometimes we get an opportunity to practice what we preach and such was the time. I was under Fred's pickup on the cold snow replacing a transmission that I had bought and paid the freight on. I could honestly recommend to Fred that he let Jesus be Lord of his life as he was an ever present help in times of trouble. We were very happy that we could get them going again. After five days with us, they were on the road again.

A few months later we got a cheque in the mail for about half of the bill. Then we heard Dorothy had an accident so we marked their bill "paid in full" as we knew they were in a real bind.

There were some who made it bad for others in a bind. There were times when I went out of my way an extra mile and sometimes two or three to help, they'd leave a cheque after a very convincing story, then put a stop payment on the cheque. But, I guess they have their reward.

Late one night, I was working on a washing machine and our closest neighbor came over to borrow my 22 rifle, to shoot a porcupine at their new place. They were trying to get moved about a mile down the road from us. After pulling quills from our dogs mouth a time or two, I knew them porkies were unwanted around the yard. So without question I got the gun for him.

What I didn't know, was that he and his wife had a disagreement and she had taken all his guns and went up to his brother's place. She told his brother he should go check on him, which he did. Thinking he was still at the old place, he went there first and didn't find him, so he came back up to the new place and there he was. He had just pointed the gun at his temple and ended his own life.

Meanwhile, I was pondering several things. Why would he want to kill a porcupine when they weren't moved there yet? He wasn't as jolly and happy as usual, but then maybe he had three flat tires that day, that could make him unhappy. All these things were going through my mind when another friend came by and we started talking about this. Then, another neighbor came by and asked where the accident was. Immediately I suspected something, we jumped in my truck and when we got there he was taking his last breath. I just stood there and thanked the Lord for the extra strength he had given me when I really needed it.

A few days later my friend came and found me working out by a picnic table, reached out his long arm and put it around my neck and said, "Jerry, don't let this bother you too much, it was not your fault." I never knew what that could mean to a person, until Richard did it to me. From that day, I learned the value of putting your arm around someone who is hurting and letting them know you care, even if you think you don't know what to say. The only thing necessary is just, "I care about you."

One morning right after we moved to Tatogga, one of our friends we had known in Alberta who now lived up the road from us came and brought a big pan of morning muffins. Dee had a big smile on her face and she said, "Welcome to the Iskut area." What a nice thing to do for a newcomer.

In September our staff told us, "We can handle this place, Jerry and Rose, you guys go do what you'd like for a few days." So, Manny, Rose and I got Murray to fly us out to a lake and leave us there for a week.

By this time Murray had become a good friend. He is one of the people who appear hard and tough, but on the inside he has a heart of gold. Our children and grandchildren fell in love with this man that flies the Beaver plane on floats.

We took everything we would need for a week, including our food, packed our back packs and started off up the mountain. I soon found this was hard work. The next day my legs felt as if they would break if they bent. It seemed like Rose had no problem with her pack, maybe it's because she's younger or it could have been the new back pack I'd gotten her for her birthday. Manny had been guiding for an outfitter for a while already and he sure made it tough for his Dad to keep him in sight.

We had a wonderful time. Two days before the plane came back to pick us up, we found a nice bull caribou about six miles beyond our camp. Manny was kind and said, "Go ahead, shoot him, Dad."

After we had skinned and boned him out, I realized then what a project we'd gotten into. Our camp seemed a long way off, down hill and on a steep side hill most of the way. Dark overtook us before we got to camp. I had to leave part of my load beside the trail until the next morning, it was just too heavy.

The next morning, Manny and Rose each took a load three miles down to the lake where we'd be picked up. I skinned out the cape and got it ready for mounting. I thought an animal that beautiful should be mounted for later enjoyment.

We were back at the lake and had seen some moose swimming in the lake and were just enjoying God's beautiful creation and the beautiful clear water, when we heard the hum of Murray's plane coming to get us. We just had to have one more cup of coffee with Murray here before we left.

We had a real welcoming committee waiting for us. The meat was great. The caribou was still in the velvet. Sure enough the staff had done a great job without us.

The outfitter that Manny was guiding for, Jerry Geraci mounted the caribou head for us and did a wonderful job.

We did many projects that summer and one of my favorite helpers was Matthew. He came to me for work soon after we moved here and we found we could work together well. We put some new tin roofs on some of the old cabins. There was always the winter wood pile to work on. We built a little honeymoon cache late in the fall. It is sitting on big poles, twelve feet off the ground. It has a great view of the mountains.

We were sort of keeping an eye out for a certain herd of mountain goats. When that project was completed, we planned to go across the lake and get one.

On October 11, our daughter in law, Joanne said, "I can handle this place today if you want to go get your goat." So, after a hearty breakfast but before day break, Matthew, Rose and I motored across the cold lake.

It was a steep climb and once we had to lie down on the mountain side to let a snow squall go by, we couldn't see a thing. Around 2:00 p.m. I shot a nice Billy. He was snow white with black horns and hooves. His hair was real long so he could lie out on those rocks in the cold wind and not freeze to death.

With it skinned and boned out, our packs felt heavy once again. Rose packed the hide as well as some of the meat. We planned to do a full mount on the animal so we left the head attached to the hide to skin out at home. We were hurrying as much as possible as the day was well spent and we weren't prepared to spend a night out there.

Matthew was a great mountain man at sixty years. He really made me sweat to keep up. He loaded some of the stomach fat on top of his pack for his dog and away we went.

Every step we took was down and on a slope. I thought my ankles and knees would surely break off. Part way down, Matthew stopped and took out the extra fat from his pack and laid it down. I asked him, "Matthew what are you doing?" He said, "I don't love my dog that much. I want to make it down to the bottom."

It was dark when we reached our boat but it had been a great day and we were ready for the nice supper Joanne had fixed.

There was a taxidermist friend there from Montana who had just come out from a hunting trip. He said, "I'll take that goat and mount it for you, life size laying on a rock for half price, if I can put my name on it as the taxidermist." So he finished skinning out the head and preparing the hide. He did a wonderful job on it. It is a beautiful work of art.

Most of the guides and outfitters close down their camps and come out around the middle of October usually. Winter is near, horse feed is gone, ice flow can start in the rivers anytime and the float planes can't land anymore to haul out the necessary gear and meat.

I think about the bank sometimes and how much money they lost from the first offer we had given them and they said, "No, that's not enough." After Rose, Annabelle and I moved out they put the land up for sale by tender, no one bid on it except our family.

Ken and Darla bought the home half back and moved into the house I'd built for Rose twenty years ago, which we think is kind of neat. My brother, Jody bought seven quarters of it and told me if I made the yearly payments on it, I could pay it out and it would be ours again. Jody's son in law, Mike bought the other half section; that meant all the land had stayed in the family. Now, we could enjoy going back for a visit or to help if we could.

Lawrence is a man who gained our respect and appreciation for he has helped us in so many ways. He was one who wasn't afraid to let his cattle graze on our place and even had them seized once for doing it. He still has the seven quarters leased for his cattle and the lease money he pays almost makes the payments for the seven quarters, so why not? Lawrence and his wife, Florence are also on the Advisory Board of the Southern Baptist Seminary in Cochrane, Alberta.

Land prices had continued to slide, so by the time the bank got their money from the land and paid legal fees for three years, they were several hundred thousand dollars short of what we first offered them. Too bad they were so bent on making an example of us and forgot about using good judgment. After our ordeal, the bank's lawyer was no longer an employee with that law firm.

On a trip to Terrace I met a Realtor who said, "You know a lot of people would like to have your Resort." We told her if someone wants it more than we do they can have it, so we listed it with her for one year.

In March 1993, Rose and I traveled to Alberta for my Dad's eightieth birthday. It was great to be with so many loved ones again.

Annabelle made us grandparents, our number twelve and her first. She presented us with sweet little baby, Trey on March 9, 1993.

While we were over that way we made our second tape with our children called "Precious Mem'ries" and our third one with each other called "You and Me." Again we were happy to work with Lorne in Fort St. John, B.C.

In May of 1993 we were all set for another busy season. Our help was all lined up. Stan and Joanne and their little family came up again to help us for the summer. We always enjoyed having our family work with us and the grandchildren are so special. Sometimes Rose felt so under pressure it was hard to show her devotion to them, there was just so much to keep her busy.

We had a woman booked to come be head cook way back in April, but she didn't have to be on duty till June first. Several people warned Rose about hiring her and she was so disappointed when she called Helen to see if everything was in order and Helen said, "Oh, I won't be coming. I can make more here." That was a hard lesson to learn, but once again Rose turned to the Lord and found out it was much better this way. He always knows best and we needed help we could count on.

Joanne came to her rescue and said, "As long as you'll help me, I'll be your head cook." What a wonderful attitude. I thought of Ruth in the Bible, who was so loyal to her mother in law. So, Joanne became our head cook for the season and there was no one who could have done the job better.

Stan was also great help. He always enjoyed mechanic work and was getting good at it. If a motor needed repairing, he could do it. Stan has always been an independent thinker, so was Columbus. He was a big help to Rose in the times I had to go to work in the bush and it was great when he got big enough to come help me in the bush, too. He was a good machinery operator and full of fun.

Stan was kind of like his older brother, Manny. He liked to see how steep a hill his snow machine could climb or how far he could jump from a high ramp on his dirt bike. He wanted to see if he could actually out run the cops on his bike one day and he did, but he found out that didn't pay. Now for him to come and help me at Tatogga was a big asset because there were so many things he could do.

Stan and I have always been able to talk about our problems. Even when he knew he was going in a wrong direction, we were able to pray together. I am so thankful for a good relationship between our sons and daughters and our in laws.

Stan had done quite a bit of auto body repair and painting, so our old tow truck got a face lift. It didn't take him long to earn a good reputation with stranded tourists.

George came into our life early in May also. I needed a helper to do electrical work, fixing and just doing lots of odd jobs and had not found anyone yet. A friend stopped in one night and said, "Here's someone I think you'll like, meet my friend, George."

George said he had dreamed all his sixty plus years of spending a summer at a Resort somewhere and said if we'd have him, all he wanted was what he ate. We took him up on it and found out we got the best end of the stick many times, as all he ever ate was popcorn and soup. What an asset and a good helper he was.

Cindy was a sweetheart to have work for us. She too came early in May dressed for work. There wasn't much she couldn't do. She mainly ran the gas bar and parked rigs in the campground and she did a super job. She was very artistic and painted several signs to brighten up the place some. All our help was just what God had chosen for us.

Tracy answered an ad Rose put in the paper for a waitress. She came right after she graduated from High School at the end of June. She had a winning smile and a good attitude. She seemed to never tire. Like Cindy there wasn't much she couldn't or wouldn't do. Sometimes running a business like this you need your help to be versatile. Tracy stayed with us until we closed for the season and took over the gas bar after Cindy left to go back to school in August.

Joan came to us along in July. She was with some other family members who had been our good friends for years. When the family prepared to depart, Joan said to Rose, "I'll stay and bake bread for you, and you don't have to pay me." Rose insisted on having home baked bread for the restaurant and she did relish the idea of a spell off, but she pretended to play hard to get so she told Joan, "I have to taste your bread first." Joan did nothing but beat it back down to her motor home and came trucking back in with a loaf of her bread. Rose told her, "You're on, Joanie" and that's how she came into our lives.

She stayed right up until the end of the season so Rose wouldn't have so much to do and what an asset she was. She not only baked bread but pies with meringue three inches thick, cookies that would melt in your mouth and all kinds of goodies. Whenever things got a little grim you could count on Joanie to get every one laughing.

We had six of our young neighbor kids from Alberta come to visit us for a week. These were, Henry, Mary, Tina, Martin, Henry, and Jake who had helped us move up here. What a great bunch to have come to visit.

While we were visiting we cut wood, stacked it, painted cabins, changed a motor in a truck, fixed flats, cut up rhubarb, baked pies, washed dishes, mowed grass and nearly every evening we went fishing. One night we even had a fishing derby, guess who caught the biggest.

It was a great year for us with so many friends and loved ones. Our own three daughters all made it up with their families and as always the way their mother had taught them, there was always something they thought they had to be doing. What great memories we have as they all pitched in with the work and had fun as they did it. We will always be grateful for the wonderful family that the Lord gave us.

So many different types of tourists passing through every day added color to our little corner of the world. We had nine different Caravans stay with us that were booked previously the winter before, with twenty to thirty rigs in each one. Sometimes Cindy had her work cut out for her, parking all those. I tried to be around when those Caravan days came as they could get hectic.

They were usually booked to have supper and sometimes breakfast; that made a lot of extra work for the cooking staff. This usually meant about seventy or so for the meal.

We have gotten so many nice cards and letters back from so many people who stayed in our campground. We also usually had a door prize for the Caravans to make their stay a little more memorable, which was usually one of our own tapes.

A lot of the people bought our tapes when they found out we had some. Our desire was always that people would get a blessing from our tapes.

We were so blessed to have my father in law, Dick spend the summer with us. A nephew, Doug Lubeck brought him up early in May. He told us he wanted to be independent, chop his own wood and carry his own water. That's just what he did. Rose fixed up a little cabin for him before he came and we called it, "Grandpa's Cabin."

He was an inspiration to us all and whenever some of the staff or grandchildren would come up missing we'd go look at Grandpa's and there they'd be. He and George got along real well and Joan was always smuggling pies over to him. Everyone called him Grandpa. Many of the natives of Iskut came to visit and learn things that he could teach them.

After things slowed down for the summer, we logged off a strip to the lake for future parking as there was getting to be more and more people wanting to stop and camp with us. What a change that made, as now you can see the lake from the campground.

We made so many new friends. We met Roger one fall when he was waiting for his nephew to come out from guiding as the season was over. The weather was just too bad for the plane to fly out so Roger was stuck at Tatogga.

The fire extinguisher inspector had turned into a fine friend. Ed had told us if we could get the new hood for over the grill that he'd come up from Terrace and help us put it in. We got the hood made in Vancouver and sent up after we had closed the restaurant down for the winter. Ed had some business in Dease Lake so on his way to his home in Terrace, he stopped in and we started on the hood installation. We soon found out he had a great love for the Lord too. He really knew how to install a hood and we had a great time.

When it came time to hook the electricity up to it, who but Roger should walk in and say, "Hey, I'll do that. I'm an electrician and I'm just killing time waiting for that doggone Gene anyway." So Roger hooked the electricity up to the hood. It is just amazing how all our needs were taken care of one by one.

The next year we wanted to clean up some electrical problems so I called Roger to come help us. I knew after the hood installing he was a good electrician. We got to know him and grew quite fond of this man. He told us he and his wife had been apart for some time.

One day he said, "My wife is flying up from Ontario, I'm going to pick her up in Vancouver and bring her up for a day or so." So we got to meet his wife, Mae. We knew then that there was no real reason for them to be apart and with God's help they could put the pieces back together and carry on.

Roger had to come back again as we were putting a much heavier service entrance in our new shop. After we finished that project he left. On Christmas Day we got a phone call from Ontario and Roger on the other end said, "Merry Christmas and guess what, me and Mae got back together again and we are going to make it work." We really learned to appreciate this man, Roger.

I have learned another good lesson down through the years. There have been many people that for different reasons have chosen to stay away from church. Like the man that wouldn't go because they wouldn't put the piano where he wanted it.

I discovered personally that if I allowed anyone to control my relationship to the Lord by what they said or didn't say to me or what they did or didn't do to me, then I was not letting the Lord be my guide and director. I had to ask Him to help me to get rid of any wrong ideas I'd been harboring and ask Him to make me what He wanted me to be.

An unforgiving spirit can stop my spiritual growth and cause my prayers to be unanswered. The same thing applies in a marriage, an unforgiving partner can wreck the relationship. My relationship to God is very important to me and I don't want anything to hinder it. I'm sad to say that when we moved away from Worsley, I had allowed myself to be hurt by my Christian friends because it seemed as though they really didn't care about our physical needs. I have realized this could totally wreck my relationship with my Lord. God showed me that I was making a tremendous mistake by holding a grudge against people. I had no business doing that. It's so easy for us humans to get caught in the trap of self pity. At that point, I begged God to forgive my wrong thoughts and actions and to please restore to me the joy of my salvation and He did.

Our friend Frog that lived in Wisconsin had cancer for over a year. Now the phone call told us he was no longer with us earthlings. I had talked to him a week ago and prayed with him over the phone and I was so happy I had done this. We had many happy times together nd enjoyed each other's companionship and friendship so much. Now, Sherry had to face the world without him. I had to shed a few tears for her.

Just two weeks prior to our listing running out the real estate lady, Sheila called and told us there were some people who were interested in buying our Resort and they would like to come and look at it.

Two weeks before this, I had called her to tell her that when the listing ran out, we would not be re listing again as we had done so many improvements and it was our plan to dig all the old fuel tanks out of the ground, get the soil tested for the Environment people, and then purchase a large environmental approved above ground tank. This big tank would have one compartment for gas and one for diesel and we had already done some research on it and found out we had to have our order in well ahead of time for it to be built in Nisku, Alberta.

We were undecided about going back to Alberta for Christmas so when Sheila called to say these people wanted to come during Christmas week, that settled that. So we put the invitation out to the family to come to Tatogga for Christmas. Rose went out and found a beautiful Balsam tree and decorated it so pretty.

None of the Alberta kids could come but Manny, Fran, Dwayne, Chris and Dustin came up from Terrace. Marvin came over and had dinner with us too.

The lake was frozen over so the snow skidooing was great, as was the ice fishing. We put a harness on our German Shepherd dog, Spike and he gave the kids several rides on the sleigh. We found we were all champions at crokinole. What a beautiful part of the world to spend Christmas and celebrate the birth of our Saviour!

It is always kind of sad when the time comes for family and friends to leave but it is always so good they came.

Hal, Bunty and Matthew came up from Terrace to look at the Resort. They liked it and made us an offer that we accepted. The offer included their house in Terrace as part payment. We decided to go ahead with the fuel tank project as planned. The agreement was signed and we were to move out and them to take over on April 15, 1994.

In the cold of February we dug the tanks out of the ground. A man from Prince Rupert came and did the soil testing and they tested good. The new fuel tank arrived here on April 10, 1994.

The new owners moved in the Resort on April 12, 1994.

Rose and I moved to the house by the lake. We spent most of the summer fixing up a good place to live.

In June, Rose and I were privileged to be a part of a hundred and twenty fifth anniversary at the Elmont Baptist Church just west of Van Alstyne, Texas. This was the place where I had said, "Yes, Jesus, I want to be one of yours," so many years ago. What a wonderful time we had with many old friends and relatives. How especially wonderful it was to get to be with my old Sunday School teacher, Sib and his family. Another highlight was to get to spend some time with my third grade teacher, Ruth.

The house in Terrace was sold in September. On December 1, 1994, the money from that sale was used to buy back the seven quarters of land in Alberta that the bank had gotten. It was a great day to have this transferred back to us, because our whole family had put in a lot of sweat and blood clearing the land, picking roots and preparing the land for production of grain and cattle. What a Hallelujah day!

"A successful hunt," 1994. Dick Dixon (author's 93 year old father - in - law), Manny Hale, Robin Freeman and Jerry Hale

Jerry on "Cactus" with dog, Rusty

146

Chapter Twenty Three
It's Really Worth It All

It's time to put another log on the fire. Rose has changed from humming to singing so I can tell she's very happy. Her life didn't come to an end after all.

We kind of wonder what our next chapter in life will be. We both feel this part of the world is where God wants us to be for now. I can't really express how grateful I am for what He has done for us.

While travelling down this life highway, I have become very grateful to my Mother. She was always kind and fair to us children. She tried to teach us things that were good for us. Mom had an intuition that was very keen..

One time I had gone with Dad to help him drive as he was making on more trip to Canada before we moved. I had gone as far as Great Falls, Montana and Dad thought that was far enough so he bought me a bus ticket back to Van Alstyne, Texas. I would take two days for me to get back home so he gave me five bucks, in case I got hungry (I was still in training). Anyway the bus stopped in Billings, Montana. The depot closed for the night as the bus would leave at 8 A:M the next morning. What a night, by 8 A:M, I must have toured most of Billings on foot. When we pulled into Van Alstyne, it was pouring down rain and in the middle of the night. There was Mom to meet me. I've often marvelled at how she knew when I'd get there. We lived in the country and had no telephone. I call that "Mother's intuition."

One day after I'd started noticing the opposite sex and had taken a girl out a time or two for a date, Mom called me aside and said, "Jerry, that girl don't have a very good look in her eye". I wasn't sure what she'd seen, but I respected her opinion and that ended that. But, my Alberta Rose passed the test. I knew I was on the right track if I had Mom's approval.

It was very hard for Mom to move to Canada away from her family. She said God told her one day that it was not an accident that they were in Worsley, but it was part of His plan. Then she said she had wonderful peace. What a wonderful thing to have a Mom as we had. She taught us children about the love of God when we were small. She was the best Mom I could have had. A Mother has such a privilege to have children. It is also a great responsibility.

My Dad has been a man of courage, strength and determination. He is a man that truly wanted to do his best for the Lord. He had a set of values and standards and as long as we were living under his roof, he enforced them. As a boy, I thought I shouldn't have gotten so many spankings but one day, he helped me to understand.

My Dad had brought my lunch out to the field one day where I was operating a self propelled Combine, on some very short grain. I got into the pickup to eat my lunch. Dad got on this Combine. He hadn't run this self propelled machine yet and thought he'd make a few rounds while I had my lunch.

He hadn't gone far when he dropped the header down too low. It dug into the ground and started to pile up dirt. All of a sudden, there were too many levers and he got exited and didn't know what to do. The pile of dirt got so big that all the boards on the reels broke off. Then the engine stalled and everything was quiet. He jumped down off the Combine, picked up a broken board and gave himself a spanking right then and there. From where I was sitting, it looked very funny to see him spanking himself on the rear, jumping around and calling himself down. But I didn't dare laugh in fear he might see me and then! When he finished he came to the truck, climbed in and said, "Well, if it had been one of you boys did that, I would have given you a spanking. It was only fair I got one". We went and got all new boards and rebuilt the reels.

At a very young age, my Dad taught me a very valuable thing. I didn't understand it until I had children of my own. I have tried to pass it on to them. I learned that I could get a spanking and then at his command, stop the crying immediately. I've noticed some people as adults have not found out they can control their emotions.

Mothers and Fathers each have such an important role to play in raising children. I would like to encourage all couples to work hard at staying together. Don't give up just because it is tough going today. Tomorrow is a brand new day. I have found it to be true that if a couple works hard together and will be honest with each other, they can over come many difficulties.

In the tough valley experiences of our life, we really need each others support. If a man knows his wife is behind him, he will take on a Lion. For you husbands who are not being the man at home, ask God to help you be that. There are some pleasurable times being missed because some women don't let the husband be the head of the home. But, when things are right, a husband would give his life for his wife and the wife would also fight a Tiger for her man. A home with children needs a Mom and Dad both very bad so sons and daughters know what's necessary to have a good marriage of their own.

We have a wonderful world to live in because our Fore Fathers were not ashamed, in fact they were proud to be called the children of God. Are you ashamed to be called one of God's children? Have you asked Him to be your strength, your Redeemer? Jesus is my best friend. I sincerely hope He is yours too. Then you won't ever have to walk alone either.

Manny, Fran and their three sons, Dwayne, Christopher, and Dustin live in Terrace, B.C.

Darla and Ken Ponath and their children, Brandon, Shandy, Kamie and Bethany live in Cleardale, Alberta on the old home place.

Lisa and Melvin Lubeck and their children, Kandice and Landi live in Fairview, Alberta.

Stanford, Joanne, and their children, Samantha, Cameron and Josee live on a farm in Cleardale, Alberta near the Ponaths.

Annabelle and Klayton Krangnes with their children, Trey and Ayla live in New Norway, Alberta.

Rose and I celebrated our thirty fifth wedding anniversary on October 24, 1994.

My brother Lewis (Blue) and his wife, Betty live on a farm near, Worsley, Alberta. They have four sons and seven grandchildren.

My brother Joseph (Jody) and his wife Brenda live on a farm near Hines Creek, Alberta. They have four daughters, one son and eight grandchildren.

My brother, Dudley K (Soup) and his wife, Brenda pastor a Baptist Church in Fairview, Alberta. They have two daughters and two grandchildren.

My sister Charlotte and her husband Bruce Parker live on a farm in Cleardale, Alberta. They have two daughters, one son and one son in law.

My brother, Dick and his wife Shirlee pastor the Baptist Church in Worsley, Alberta. They have three sons and three daughters.

These are all original mates.

My Dad and Mother are now retired and live in Fairview, Alberta. They originally settled in Worsley where they farmed after moving from Texas in 1957. My Dad started the Worsley Baptist Church as a Mission out of Edmonton in the early sixties. He pastored there for twenty some years and then started the Mission in Fairview in the eighties.

He sold the farm to Dick and Shirlee and he and Mother moved to Fairview in 1987. He turned eighty one in March 1994 and still has some cattle he likes to play with. My Mother enjoys living in town. She turned seventy five in September 1994.

The family has grown from seven in 1957 to sixty nine in 1994.

Rose's Dad, Willis still makes his home in the Homesteader Lodge in Hines Creek, Alberta. He has an active memory and claims his main job in the lodge is to look after the "old People."

He turned ninety two on September 26, 1994. Lots of his family from near and far came to help him celebrate his birthday down at Many Islands, one of his favorite places beside the great Peace River. He truly still has a pioneer spirit with a real love for the Lord.

Rose's Mom, Florence passed away on October 22, 1989, at the age of seventy six. She too had a real pioneer spirit and her love for her children and her Lord was great.

Rose has three brothers living, four sisters, three brother in laws, three sister in laws and many nieces and nephews.

The scenery out our dining room window is very beautiful. It overlooks Tatogga Lake which is now frozen and under a blanket of snow. The majestic mountains towering high above the lake magnify God's handiwork. In the summer time we can often watch the mountain goats. Sometimes we even see mountain sheep from our window. What a wonderful place to live.

God truly is good!

Jerry and Rose Hale, their children and their spouses
(L to R:) Joanne, Stan, Darla, Ken, Rose, Jerry,
Klayton, Annabelle, Manny, Fran, Mel, Lisa

Order Form

I Never Walked Alone can be obtained from:

Jerry and Rose Hale
Box 233
Worsley, Ab.
T0H 3W0

Box 116
Iskut, B.C.
V0J 1K0

Name ————————————————————————

Address ————————————————————————

City ———————————— Province ——————————

Postal Code ——————————————

Enclosed is my check for:

$16.95 per book x ———— books = ————

(includes shipping & handling)

GST (if applicable) ————

PST (if applicable) ————

Total = ————

Autographed copy?   Yes ☐   No ☐

Please allow 4-6 weeks for delivery
Orders must be prepaid; no C.O.D.'s
please write to ask about quantity discounts
or public speaking engagements